*DER NIEDERRHEINISCHE
ORIENTBERICHT, c. 1350*

Der Niederrheinische Orientbericht, c. 1350

An Account of the Oriental World by an Anonymous Low German Writer

Translated with a Commentary by
Albrecht Classen

D. S. BREWER

© Albrecht Classen 2024

All Rights Reserved. Except as permitted under current legislation
no part of this work may be photocopied, stored in a retrieval system,
published, performed in public, adapted, broadcast,
transmitted, recorded or reproduced in any form or by any means,
without the prior permission of the copyright owner

The right of Albrecht Classen to be identified as
the author of this work has been asserted in accordance with
sections 77 and 78 of the Copyright, Designs and Patents Act 1988

First published 2024
D. S. Brewer, Cambridge

ISBN 978 1 84384 690 1

D. S. Brewer is an imprint of Boydell & Brewer Ltd
PO Box 9, Woodbridge, Suffolk IP12 3DF, UK
and of Boydell & Brewer Inc.
668 Mt Hope Avenue, Rochester, NY 14620–2731, USA
website: www.boydellandbrewer.co.uk

A CIP catalogue record for this book is available
from the British Library

The publisher has no responsibility for the continued existence or accuracy of URLs
for external or third-party internet websites referred to in this book, and does not
guarantee that any content on such websites is, or will remain, accurate or appropriate

CONTENTS

Acknowledgements	vii
Introduction	1
Translation	15
Commentary	83
Appendix: Sample Pages of the Original Manuscript to Illustrate the Author's Middle Low German Language	133
Bibliography of Works Consulted	135
Index	145

ACKNOWLEDGEMENTS

It is my pleasure to express my gratitude to the University of Arizona for granting me a sabbatical in Fall semester of 2022 and to the Binational US Fulbright Commission for providing a grant to carry out research and to teach at Cairo University from September to December 2022.[1] During that period, I was able to complete the translation and verify most of the specific names of plants and historical figures. The time spent in Cairo made it possible to visit some of the medieval sites and so have a better impression of what our author must have seen himself in terms of the local architecture, fauna, and flora. The splendor of the medieval buildings, though often covered today by the unavoidable Saharan dust, is still clearly apparent and left a deep impression on me.

Years ago, my former student, Carolin Radtke, was the first to trigger my interest in this account. She wanted to write her doctoral dissertation on the *Niederrheinische Orientbericht*, translating the medieval text into modern German, but her career plans prevented her from doing that. So, I have picked up this 'baton' and would like to express my gratitude to her for this inspiration. My wife Carolyn read through the entire translation and offered valuable input, confirming the curiosity that this text could arouse for a wider audience. My colleague Thomas Willard, also at the University of Arizona, was kind enough to read portions of the manuscripts and make some suggestions. I am also grateful to my colleague Carlee Arnett, University of California, Davis, for helpful comments. Further thanks go to a historian colleague at Cairo University, Emad Aboghazi, who discussed some of the aspects of Mamluk history with me, though the Arabic sources remain rather ambiguous and do not help much to shed more light on some of the details presented by the anonymous author. David S. Bachrach, University of New Hampshire, was kind enough to read the manuscript in its penultimate version and to recommend it to the publisher for publication. Marilyn Sandidge, Westfield State College, MA, generously lent her help in looking over the text one more time to clean up some unidiomatic passages. I am

---

[1] I gave a brief talk on my research, "A Fourteenth-Century German Rhinelander Observing the Middle East: New Perspectives for the Global Middle Ages," at the *2022 Annual Fulbright-Egypt Alumni Conference*, Cairo, Egypt, Oct. 2022. I am grateful for that opportunity.

Acknowledgements

also grateful to several anonymous readers whom the publisher involved at various last stages. Last but not least, Caroline Palmer from Boydell & Brewer deserves my deep gratitude for her interest in this translation project and her help in steering it through the review and final editing process. I could not have had a better editor and am deeply indebted to her.

INTRODUCTION

MEDIEVAL TRAVELERS AND THEIR ACCOUNTS

Recent research has deeply engaged with the vast corpus of medieval and early modern travel and pilgrimage literature, published both in the West and in the East. People in Latinate Europe during the Middle Ages were much on the road, contrary to many modern assumptions, and often covered huge distances. Arabic travelers, however, though also going on huge journeys, such as Ibn Fadlan (879–960), Ibn Jubayr (1145–1217), Ibn Battuta (1304–1368/1369), or Yāqūt Shihāb al-Dīn ibn-ʿAbdullāh al-Rūmī al-Ḥamawī (1179–1229), tended not to approach or touch on Christian European territory, apart from Andalusia (southern Spain) and Sicily (across from Tunisia). There were, of course, also Indian or Chinese travelers, but my knowledge about them is too limited to engage with them here.

Marco Polo (c. 1254–c. 1324), with his *Travels* (c. 1300), also known as *Book of the Marvels of the World,* and *Il Milione,* and in the original Franco-Venetian as *Devisement du Monde,* composed with the courtly poet Rustichello da Pisa, is of course well-known among medievalists and arguably even to a wider audience to this very day, being recognized as a fascinating and daring author. Children in the USA, for instance, commonly play a game based on the name of Marco Polo. Numerous travel companies use his name for their own purpose, and "Polo" has to serve even for video chat apps.

As famous as Polo's work already was during the late Middle Ages, the "armchair traveler" John Mandeville achieved much wider popularity with his own *Travels,* although, or perhaps because, fact and fiction intermingle here in a brilliant fashion. As much as Mandeville claimed authority and hence authenticity, he was really more an imaginative writer than an actual traveler.[1] However, his willingness to entertain his audience with much

---

[1]   Albrecht Classen, "Marco Polo and John Mandeville: The Traveler as Authority Figure, the Real and the Imaginary," *Authorities in the Middle Ages: Influence, Legitimacy, and Power in Medieval Society,* ed. Sini Kangas, Mia Korpiola, and Tuija Aionen. Fundamentals of Medieval and Early Modern Culture, 12 (Berlin and Boston: Walter de Gruyter, 2013), 239–48. Marco Polo, *Le Devisement du monde,* ed. critique Philippe Ménard. 6 vols. Textes Littéraires Français (Geneva: Librairie Droz,

monster lore about the world in the East piqued the general interest, and many other writers followed his pattern long into the early modern age.[2] Mandeville, however, was neither the first literary author to draw on this topic nor the last, as the current translation clearly indicates.

A NEW VOICE FROM FOURTEENTH-CENTURY GERMANY

Previous scholarship has uncovered a wide range of medieval travelogues, editing and analyzing them and often also translating individual narratives.[3] The present volume adds a truly unusual voice to the gamut of available accounts now in English translation. It is not a travelogue in the narrow sense of the word; instead, we could categorize it as a learned report about the world of the Near and Middle East, maybe as an account produced by a diplomat for the archbishop of Cologne or another figure of authority from that area. We do not know the author's name and can only guess his motivations for spending so much time abroad. This writer probably came from Cologne, situated on the bank of the river Rhine, though it is just possible (yet rather unlikely) that he hailed from Aachen, i.e., northwestern Germany, near the modern border with the Netherlands. At any rate, he was a speaker of Middle Low German (northern), which shows many

---

2001–2009). For a new bilingual edition of Mandeville's text, see *Le livre de Jean de Mandeville*. Éd. bilingue, établie, traduite, présentée et annotée par Michèle Guéret-Laferté et Laurence Harf-Lancner. Champion Classiques. Série "Moyen Âge", 57 (Paris: Champion Classiques, Honoré Champion, 2023).

[2] See, for instance, Iain Macleod Higgins, *Writing East: The "Travels" of Sir John Mandeville*. The Middle Ages Series (Philadelphia, PA: University of Pennsylvania Press, 1997); Rosemary Tzanaki, *Mandeville's Medieval Audiences: A Study on the Reception of the Book of Sir John Mandeville (1371-1550)* (Aldershot, Hampshire: Ashgate, 2003); Geraldine Heng, *Empire of Magic: Medieval Romance and the Politics of Cultural Fantasy* (New York and Chichester: Columbia University Press, 2003), 239–305. See also the contributions to *Jean de Mandeville in Europa: neue Perspektiven in der Reiseliteraturforschung*, ed. Ernst Bremer and Susanne Röhl. Mittelalter-Studien, 12 (Paderborn: Wilhelm Fink, 2007). The literature on Polo and Mandeville is vast, which underscores the importance of their travelogues as identified by modern research. Most recently, see Simon Gaunt, *Marco Polo's* Le devisement du monde: *Narrative Voice, Language and Diversity*. Gallica, 31 (2013; Cambridge: D. S. Brewer, 2018).

[3] The accounts by Marco Polo and John Mandeville are commonly known, but now we also have available a critical edition of Odorico da Pordenone, *Relatio de Mirabilibus Orientalium Tatarorum*. Edizione critica a cura di Annalia Marchisio (Florence: SISMEL, Edizioni del Galluzzo, 2016). Other scholars have busily worked at editing Arabic, Indian, or Chinese travelogues. There is no room here for an extensive bibliographical overview.

Introduction

similarities with Middle Dutch, and is very distinct from Middle High German (southern).[4]

We have no clear idea about his social status or biography, and we must rely for our knowledge of him on just two manuscripts containing his text, the *Niederrheinische Orientbericht* (*An Account of the Oriental World by An Anonymous Low German Writer*). Contrary to some comments by Brall-Tuchel,[5] the editor of one of the manuscripts and translator of the text into modern German, the author cannot have been a Jew, since he describes the Jews living in Egypt and elsewhere with either disrespect or just a lack of interest, simply listing the various subgroups and their customs without indicating any form of identification with them. Even if the author had been a Jew in his youth and had subsequently converted to Christianity, which would be pure speculation, he does not reflect on his past and present religion. Rather, he espouses a very traditional, sober Catholicism, without any uncertainty or doubts. He does not seem to have been a merchant either, because he only mentions certain market conditions in the East and typical trading goods in passing.

His many comments on the court and the conditions in Egypt and elsewhere strongly suggest that he was well connected with the local nobility and that he himself probably enjoyed the status of an aristocrat. Some of his greatest interests pertained to the different types of courtly entertainment (falconing, hunting with dogs, fishing with birds of prey, performances by acrobats, dances, presentation of exotic animals, etc.), but he hardly pays any attention to the ordinary people in the cities, such as craftsmen, or the peasantry.[6]

---

[4] Recent research has turned its attention to the individual and independent status of Low German culture, literature, and language, but the *Niederrheinische Orientbericht* has not yet been fully recognized as a major textual document of that world. See, for instance, the contributions to *Von Widukind zur ›Sassine‹: Prozesse der Konstruktion und Transformation regionaler Identität im norddeutschen Raum*, ed. Martin Baisch, Malena Ratzke, and Regina Toepfer. Forschungen zur Kunst, Geschichte und Literatur des Mittelalters, 4 (Vienna and Cologne: Böhlau, 2023). Cf. my review in *German History* (online) at: https://doi.org/10.1093/gerhis/ghad051. For the use of Low German in northern German cities, see now the contributions to *Sprachgeschichte vor Ort: Stadtsprachenforschung im Spannungsfeld zwischen Ortspunkt und Sprachraum*, ed. Matthias Schulz and Lukas Kütt (Heidelberg: Universitätsverlag Winter, 2022).

[5] *Von Christen, Juden und von Heiden: Der niederrheinische Orientbericht*, ed., trans., and commentary by Helmut Brall-Tuchel. Unter Mitarbeit von Jana Katczynski, Verena Rheinberg, and Sarafina Yamoah (Göttingen: V & R unipress, 2019).

[6] Albrecht Classen, "Entertainment and Recreation in Medieval Courtly Society: Literary, Historical, and Art-Historical Perspectives," forthcoming in *Groniek: Historisch Tijdschrift*.

While he spent a long time in the Near and Middle East, his purpose was not that of a pilgrim, since he does not display any particular interest in religious sites apart from some general remarks about the appearance of the representatives of various Churches, who were in the presence of the Sultan to pay their respects to him. His close association with the Mamluk court in Cairo and his extensive interest in the history of Armenia, Georgia, and other kingdoms and empires might suggest that he served as a kind of diplomat or representative of a major trading company, who was either independently wealthy or was well paid for his office by his lords back home in Germany.

The anonymous author was particularly concerned with collecting as much specific information about the world in the Near and Middle East as possible to inform his audience (or his patron back home) about cultural conditions, particularly in Egypt. He demonstrates a high level of learning, though he was probably not a scholar or academically trained – there are no Latin phrases or quotes in his text, no references to any famous intellectuals or travelogue authors, and no discussions of political conflicts between the western powers and the Muslim world. Moreover, the narrative does not include any hints of ancient or medieval sources that might have been consulted, even though some can be identified.[7] This makes our assumptions about his professional status even more difficult since our author would probably have written the entire account in Latin if he had intended it as a learned treatise for university colleagues and students. His foci are the geographical conditions, the political situations, the courtly culture in Cairo, and the fauna and flora in that part of the world. It is a most informative, strikingly authentic text, fairly free of personal bias in religious terms, and based to a considerable extent on personal observations.

From a number of internal references, we can date this work to around 1350 or a little later (see also below for further arguments in favor of this dating). For instance, he refers to a pogrom against Jews that took place in Cologne in 1349. He also briefly remarks on the Hundred Years' War between England and France as being in the past – it began in 1337 with the Edwardian War (until 1360); however, it ended completely only in c. 1451, with both sides experiencing victories and defeats – but he does not engage with any specifics. We can be certain that the writer lived somewhere in the Middle East, or 'Orient,' as he calls it, for at least a dozen years, spending much time in Egypt in particular, and in neighboring countries or regions.

---

[7] See now the contributions to *Travel, Time, and Space in the Middle Ages and Early Modern Time: Explorations of Worldly Perceptions and Processes of Identity Formation*, ed. Albrecht Classen. Fundamentals of Medieval and Early Modern Culture, 22 (Berlin and Boston: Walter de Gruyter, 2018).

Introduction

His perspectives on that world represent some of the most authentic observations by a European eyewitness and author from that time period and so deserve our close attention.

To summarize, in notable contrast to Marco Polo, our author disregarded most topics of interest to merchants, and was not a religious ambassador like the famous Franciscan missionary Odorico da Pordenone (1286–1331). Nor was he a particularly devout Christian. Instead, he reported his experiences at the Sultan's court in great detail, and living conditions in Egypt, the Holy Land, Syria, and other places. Even Persia, India, and Mongolia figure here to some extent, but it seems unlikely that he really traveled to those distant countries. However, we cannot entirely exclude that possibility, since it was fairly easy for a tourist – admittedly a rather anachronistic term for the pre-modern world – or, more likely, a diplomat to travel the entire Middle East during the mid-fourteenth century. In many ways, we can consider this report as a direct reflection of global awareness in the pre-modern world.[8]

As already noted, this author discusses a very wide range of topics, particularly aspects pertaining to the courtly world in Egypt, hunting with birds of prey, horses, weapons, clothing, foodstuffs, religion, architecture, music, politics, public ceremonies, and the fauna and flora found in that country and in neighboring regions. In a way, this author drew, as all medieval writers tended to do, including Marco Polo – and arguably modern travel authors continue to follow that pattern as well – from many earlier learned treatises and combined the factual with the fantastic. But in many respects, the former dominates the latter, as we can tell based on the accuracy of the author's comments concerning the political aspects, architecture, history, and natural environment.

There are some interesting parallels between the latter section of our author's text dealing with the flora in the Near and Middle East and the natural encyclopedia by Konrad von Megenberg (1309–1374), his *puoch von den naturleichen dingen* (begun in c. 1349; "The Book of Natural Things"), such as the passage on the aloe tree (IV/B2). Konrad, who originated from Bavaria, partially based his treatise on Thomas de Cantimpré's *Liber de natura rerum* in its German version from c. 1270, but he might have certainly drawn from the wider tradition of natural encyclopedias composed in Latin, such as Vincent of Beauvais's *Speculum naturale* or

---

[8]   See now Albrecht Classen, "Globalism in the Late Middle Ages: The Low German *Niederrheinische Orientbericht* as a Significant Outpost of a Paradigm Shift. The Move Away from Traditional Eurocentrism," *Globalism in the Middle Ages and the Early Modern Age: Innovative Approaches and Perspectives*, ed. Albrecht Classen. Fundamentals of Medieval and Early Modern Culture, 27 (Berlin and Boston: Walter de Gruyter, 2023), 381–406.

Bartholomew Anglicus's *De proprietatibus rerum*, both active in the thirteenth century.[9]

Recent years have witnessed a sudden emergence of new attention dedicated to our Low German author and his account. Although he is certainly not the most accomplished writer – there are at times weaknesses in his style and repetitions, his syntax is occasionally faulty, and there are numerous passages where he makes a rather clumsy attempt to render the local names into Middle Low German – his narrative deserves to be fully acknowledged as an extraordinary late medieval account about the Near East. He frequently seems to have filled gaps in his knowledge from some learned sources, or simply invented things, as many of his contemporaries did. As is to be expected, for instance, we find references to 'classical' monster lore without any effort to verify remarks about the various types of creatures which resemble the human race only partially.

At the same time, the author is strikingly committed to reflecting on the various religions he encountered with an open mind. Occasionally, he goes so far as to recognize 'otherness' as a common feature which differentiates people but does not alienate them from each other. Not unexpectedly, though, as a western Christian, he tends to belittle various Christian sects in the East (Greek Orthodox, Nestorians, etc.) as inferior in their faith, calling them regularly 'bad Christians.' He also has much to say about Islam and Judaism, but he commonly notes that the various representatives of all three religions were fully entitled to participate in the Sultan's courtly life, were apparently respected in their own religion, and were treated mostly on equal terms.

The author appears to have had an excellent command of the material/ information that he conveyed. We cannot tell what level of linguistic skills he had in Arabic or Syrian Aramaic, Turkish or Persian, but the entire report suggests personal experiences and a high level of comfort with foreign languages, religions, and cultures. Judging by what we know of many late medieval pilgrimage authors, such as Bernhard von Brey[or: i]denbach (c. 1440–1497), either Italian or French was the *lingua franca* in the Middle East, but we cannot exclude the possibility that our author might also have acquired sufficient knowledge of the local languages to communicate with ease, at least within courtly circles. He proves to be an astoundingly well-informed, highly curious eyewitness and also a more or less learned author, with access to important chronicle literature about some of the

---

[9] Gerold Hayer, *Konrad von Megenberg, 'Das Buch der Natur': Untersuchungen zu seiner Text- und* Überlieferungsgeschichte. Münchener Texte und Untersuchungen zur deutschen Literatur des Mittelalters, 110 (Tübingen: Max Niemeyer, 1998), 8–9. Konrad von Megenberg, *Das Buch der Natur*. Vol. II: *Kritischer Text nach den Handschriften*, ed. Robert Luff and Georg Steer (Tübingen: Max Niemeyer, 2003).

Van der danckberlichen vnd eren des ewigen godes vnd den heilgen drijn Conïgen vnd de edelen godes doneren de m dir su su hen-
prehen Dar dn dat mege geschein Jnd de heilige drijveldicheit in sein
Mir volkomender selicheit des borliene vnd allen de eristheit
der vader ind der sun vnd des heiligen geistes namen Dar dat wan
werde des spricht alle amen

Er na dat geschreuen is van dem heiligen lande vnd van
allen landen van ouer mer vnd van burgen ind van steden
de da ymme gestanden inde noch steint Nu volget her na
dat Conïge vrijsten ind heren vnd bisschopen ebde
Canonissche vnd paffen ind mumche vnd wilcher hande lude da hant
geheent vnd noch wonnent bis by desen dach vnd van yrme gelou-
nen ind partien vnd van all yrme wesen van cristen Joden vnd van
heiden. Zo dem ersten dat Conickrich van Jherusalem liget mijz
in der werelde als man he spricht vnd dat hat van alders gewest-
der Joden vnd dar na was it der cristen vnd nu is it der heiden ouer
m dem Conickrich wonnent alde meist cristen. Vort van desme
Conickrich mrgain dat oisten da sint alle de Conickrich van India da
it here ouer prester Jahan vnd alle de lude de da ymme wonnent
se sint cristen. Vort mrgain dat sijd oyst by India vint alle
Conickrich van Nubien vnd dat Conickrich van Tharsin vnd da lude
sint ouch cristen Jnd danne waren Melchior ind Balthasar sheren
van den heiligen drij Conïgen de vnsem heren den offer brachten Zo
Bethleem Vort mrgain dat Norden oyst liget dat Conickrich van

Ms. W*3, Fol. 116r. Stadt Köln, Historisches Archiv und Rheinisches Bildarchiv,
Vormoderne Bestände / Nachlässe und Sammlungen, HAStK, Best. 7020, 3);
with permission.

Ms. W*3, Fol. 116v. Stadt Köln, Historisches Archiv und Rheinisches Bildarchiv, Vormoderne Bestände / Nachlässe und Sammlungen, HAStK, Best. 7020, 3); with permission.

Introduction

northern kingdoms such as Georgia and Armenia, and also Persia, India, and Mongolia.[10] When it comes to Egypt, however, there is no doubt that much of the account is, finally, based on his personal observations.

However, he has nothing to say about the educated elite, the scribes, authors, and writers at the Cairo court or anywhere else. One reason for this surprising fact might be that he was not a particularly learned person. He wrote only in Middle Low German, and not in Latin, so it is rather likely that he lacked the necessary education to make contacts or to communicate with the scholars and teachers at the Mamluk court.[11] The same, however, also applies to fifteenth-century writers who visited Cairo, such as Felix Fabri (1441–1502; a Franciscan priest who mostly wrote in Latin) and Arnold von Harff (1471–1505, a knight, who also wrote in Middle Low German). Unfortunately, this complicates the question of the biography of our anonymous author even further.

MANUSCRIPTS

Our text has survived in two manuscripts, both housed in the *Historisches Archiv der Stadt* [Historical Archive of the City] of Cologne: 1. Best. 7010 (W) 261a (1408; containing seventy-two folios still extant; the other text included here is the *Historia trium regum* [History of the Three Holy Magi] by Johannes von Hildesheim); and 2. Best. 7020 (W*3) (c. 1410–1420; the other texts contained are: Meister Wichwolt's [formerly identified as Babiloth] *Cronica Alexandri des grossen konigs*; Johannes von Hildesheim's *Historia trium regum*; *Streitgespräch zwischen Christ und Jude* [Dispute between a Christian and a Jew]; Konrad von Würzburg's *Trojanerkrieg* (excerpt: v. 19661–20054; Trojan War); *Seelentrost / Kleiner Seelentrost* [Consolation for the Soul / Small Consolation for the Soul]; *Morant und Galie*; and Bruder Philipp's *Marienleben* [Life of the Virgin Mary].[12] We cannot tell why the *Niederrheinische Orientbericht* did not enjoy a wider

---

[10] For a brief but succinct summary of the more or less current state of research, along with a good bibliography, see also Bruno Jahn, "Niederrheinische Orientbericht," *Deutsches Literatur-Lexikon: Das Mittelalter*, ed. Wolfgang Achnitz. Vol. 3: *Reiseber-ichte und Geschichtsdichtung* (Berlin and Boston: Walter de Gruyter, 2012), 170–71. For the most up to date research, see Brall-Tuchel and Micklin respectively.

[11] See, for instance, the contributions to *Court Cultures in the Muslim World: Seventh to Nineteenth Centuries*, ed. Albrecht Fuess and Jan-Peter Hartung. SOAS/Routledge Studies on the Middle East, 13 (London and New York: Routledge, 2011); Jonathan Porter Berkey, *The Transmission of Knowledge in Medieval Cairo: A Social History of Islamic Education* (Princeton, NJ: Princeton University Press, 2014).

[12] We are fortunate that these two manuscripts survived a major accident when the Historical Archive of the city of Cologne, along with two neighboring houses, collapsed on March 9, 2009, as a result of subway construction nearby.

dissemination, especially considering the enormous success of the more or less contemporary *Travels* by Marco Polo and the later narrative by John Mandeville with the same title.[13] It might be that our author's account was not fantastic enough for the contemporary audience, and represented the eastern world in terms that were too concrete and sober to appeal to a wider readership. But it might also have been the case that the author composed it solely for the archbishop of Cologne, or a secular authority, who had it then stored away, preventing the public from learning about it.

EDITIONS

After Brall-Tuchel had published his edition of the text alongside a modern German translation, Anja Micklin brought out a critical edition, printing both manuscript versions on facing pages, relying on a diplomatic reproduction of the respective text. Brall-Tuchel used the manuscript W*3; he abstained from significant interventions into the text but adapted it slightly with regard to the capitalization of names, the use of punctuation, the capitalization of first letters in new sentences, and the spelling out of abbreviations. I prefer Brall-Tuchel's pragmatic solution for the purpose of a translation, but the reader needs to keep in mind that there can be some notable, if not fundamental, differences between the three versions. One small example should suffice to illustrate this. When the anonymous author turns to the kingdom of Armenia, we observe these variants:

Ms. W261a (fol. 29r)	Ms. W*3 (fol. 121v-122r)	Brall-Tuchel's version
vort dat koninckrijch van <u>armenyen</u> lijcht recht van <u>damasco</u> bis an <u>antiochien</u> ind heyscht an der eynre sijden des souldayns / ind ander sijde/ des <u>turken</u> lant ind hait bij der dirder sijden <u>tartarijen</u> ind bij der virder sijden dat mer lijgen.	Vort dat Conickrich van Armenien recket van damasco bis zo antioichia vnd hat by der eynre siden den Soldain vnd by der andern siden de Turcken vnd by der dirden siden de Tatteren vnd by der veirden siden dat mer.	Vort dat conickrich van Armenien recket van Damasco bis zo Antioichia und hat by der eynre siden den soldain und by der anderen siden de Turcken und by der dirden siden de Tatteren und by der veirden siden dat mer.

[13] See https://www.handschriftencensus.de/werke/2380 (last accessed on Oct. 21, 2022). The manuscripts have also been described and discussed at length by Brall-Tuchel and then Micklin in their editions and translation; see below.

Introduction

The two versions replicated here in the first two columns are from Micklin's edition. Brall-Tuchel has made a considerable effort to enable the modern reader to understand the text more easily, but the differences are minimal and not crucial at all for the translation. Fortunately, Micklin's critical edition makes the text of both manuscripts available diplomatically. I have greatly profited from her work as well because it allowed me to compare both manuscript versions during the translation process. For philological issues the reader should consult the texts in the original manuscripts as reproduced by Micklin. Her edition, however, presents the two manuscripts without any subheadings or chapter titles, since they do not exist in the manuscripts.

Brall-Tuchel adds the folio pagination on the right margin of his edition, and Micklin on the left margin (for ms. W*3). Without those references, it is difficult at times to identify specific passages quickly. Brall-Tuchel offers a useful index and includes a helpful table of contents that lists those aspects in detail, which Micklin does not because her focus rests on the historical–linguistic analysis of the text. The one major drawback of Brall-Tuchel's edition is that the entire text is simply run together, whereas the original is divided into paragraphs, as Micklin replicates it in her edition.

ON THE TRANSLATION AND THE FACTUAL INFORMATION CONTAINED IN THE TEXT

Not everything the anonymous author discusses about the conditions in Egypt is completely factual or correct, as far as we can tell today. Nevertheless, the wealth of detail is certainly impressive, with the narrator taking us by virtue of his account into the local gardens and plantations, although it proves at times to be very difficult to identify the specific plants or fruits because of the Middle Low German terms used. In one case, for instance, the author identifies a type of fruit with an odd name which turns out to be a *hapax legomenon* in Middle Low and Middle High German, that is, a word extant only in these two manuscripts. Turning away from the standard dictionaries for those two languages (*Lexer*, etc.) and consulting the *Oxford English Dictionary*, however, helped me to solve the problem because the term was derived from Old French and so also entered the English language of that time. As is always the case with translations from medieval texts, some flexibility is required and hence also thinking outside the linguistic box.

Since the author appears to have been a little careless with the syntax of his narrative, it has often been necessary for the present purpose to render the meaning in a more comprehensible form instead of translating word for word, or literally according to the author's own syntax. I indicate in the notes where I have used a more fluid translation to stay as close as possible to the original meaning while rendering it adequately into modern American English. In other words, I have tried to steer clear of the Scylla of a too literal and hence unidiomatic translation and of the Charybdis of a too loose or free rendering of the original text. The translation aims to be as authentic as necessary without losing the idiomatic touch.

Real historical problems emerged in determining which Mamluk ruler/s and emirs were meant in the text, even though the author provides us with some names and even dates. While my focus here rests, of course, on the translation itself, I have aimed to research the historical background and to identify what people, fruits, trees, other plants, birds, or animals the author is discussing. In some cases, I have offered different interpretations to those provided by Brall-Tuchel in the modern German translation. Of course, that required intensive exploration of a variety of subject matters, including history, botany, biology, geography, ornithology, etc., and so the reader will find in the commentary a major body of background information for our text relevant for historians, cultural historians, religious scholars, and other researchers. This also includes comments on local currency, saints' feast days, pogroms, military conflicts, types of birds of prey for hunting, fashion, etc. Occasionally, to prevent the reader from having to turn to the footnotes and back again, I have added brief explanations or expansions in the text within square brackets to clarify the meaning.

The apparatus in the notes is intended both for the general reader who might need clarification about the canonical hours, for instance, or currency used in the Levant and nearby regions, and for a more academic audience, such as the historical philologist, for example, interested in linguistic problems and translation questions, and the literary-historical researcher. We must, however, keep in mind that the author tended to write down names of peoples, cities, rulers, animals, birds, or plants as he heard them, which has made the entire translation process into a kind of detective work, not least because previous research has not been concerned with those issues to the extent I consider necessary.[14]

---

[14] For recent and far-reaching theoretical reflections on what translating might mean, particularly within the context of philosophical texts, see now Sool Park, *Paradoxien der Grenzsprache und das Problem der Übersetzung. Eine Studie zur Textualität philosophischer Texte und zu historischen Übersetzungsstrategien* (Würzburg: Königshausen & Neumann, 2022); and for a valuable review, see Christophe Fricker online in *literaturkritik.de* (April 4, 2023), at: https://literaturkritik.de/public/rezension.php?rez_id=29606 (last accessed on April 9, 2023). As Fricker emphasizes, meaning is created through an inner-linguistic differentiation within a space beyond languages. However, bringing this all down to a pragmatic level, translating a text still means to work meticulously with words and sentences, hence the grammar,

Introduction

I would like to acknowledge the crucial help that the modern German translation by Brall-Tuchel provided for my English translation. However, I did not feel it advisable simply to rely on his edition and translation. Thus, I drew from the Middle Low German text as edited by Micklin, comparing it closely with Brall-Tuchel's edition. The extensive endnotes explicitly point out what problems I encountered and illustrate how I approached or solved them. They are both quick references and extensive commentary, depending on the circumstances. I have followed (in translation) the subheadings provided by Brall-Tuchel since they structure the text usefully.

DATING: DETAILS

The combination of the facts (names, dates, events) mentioned by the anonymous writer and the historical research that I could carry out leads me to conclude finally, despite some remaining uncertainty, that the author really originated, as claimed above, from Cologne, although he was also familiar with Aachen, and that he composed his treatise considerably later than in the early 1340s. To summarize, all indications point to a time of c. 1350 to 1360, most likely to 1352 or 1354. One of many indicators is that he refers to the year 1341 when the Black Death began to rage in the Muslim world (Brall-Tuchel, p. 86) as an event that had happened in the past. And the author also discusses the wedding of a Sultan in 1348 (Brall-Tuchel, p. 100), which seems to be the correct date, as I outline in my comments regarding this passage below, especially in light of the dynastic history of the Egyptian Mamluks. We are also informed about the Byzantine civil war from 1341 to 1347 (Brall-Tuchel, p. 124), which clearly pushes the date of composition of this treatise to after 1347. Again, the specific details supporting this conclusion are included in many of the endnotes to the translation. From a historical point of view, this all amounts to a critical evaluation of the sources which allows us to compare their information with what our author has to say.

Unfortunately, despite some good evidence, much remains uncertain. Ultimately, firm conclusions are almost impossible, since the anonymous author composed his treatise either over the course of years and/or reflected upon earlier events as he had heard them. Hence, I do not think that it would be useful to set out the various comments and arguments regarding the early or late date at this point because they are either contradictory,

---

and semantics. Hence, for my purposes, there is no need for further philosophical considerations; instead, I pursue here a straightforward approach, accepting that in translating there is always the need to compromise, adapt, and also explain the justification for a certain strategy or method.

pertain to rather different issues (political, religious, economic, military), or are too convoluted to be helpful here. However, to revisit some of the critical issues and to expand on them again because it is so important for dating, the anonymous author refers at one point to the pogrom against the Jewish population in Cologne on the night of August 23 to 24, 1349. It would have been virtually impossible for him to have learned about this terrible event while he was still in the Near East. So he could have referred to it only after having returned home and being told what had happened in Cologne during his long absence, maybe in the early 1350s. He also includes a reference to the Hundred Years' War that began in 1337. Finally, the various references to the ruling Sultan in Cairo lend further evidence to the argument that this report was composed around or well after 1350.

Altogether, this anonymous author deserves our full attention as a highly unusual voice from the mid-fourteenth century who lived for years in the Middle East, enjoying high respect at the Mamluk court. His Low German account represents firm evidence that there was considerable traffic between Latinate Europe and the Islamic world during the late Middle Ages.

TRANSLATION

THE ANONYMOUS AUTHOR'S
INTRODUCTION[1]

ENGLISH TRANSLATION: THE TEXT

In the following report, you can read about the Holy Land and all the lands of Outremer [beyond the sea],[2] and about the castles and cities that have been located there and are still standing there, then about the kings, dukes, lords, and patriarchs, bishops, abbots, canons, priests, monks, and all kinds of other people who lived there and still live there to this day, and about their faiths and religious sects, and about their culture, that is about Christians, Jews, and heathens [Muslims].[3]

Outline

First of all, there is the kingdom of Jerusalem which is situated in the middle of the world, as has been observed in the past, which used to belong to the Jews, then to the Christians, and now to the Muslims. In that kingdom, most people are Christians. Turning from that kingdom to the east, there are all those kingdoms of India that are ruled by Prester John, and all the people who live there are Christians.[4] Turning further east, there are the kingdoms of Nubia and Tharsin, and the people who live there are also Christians.[5] Melchior and Balthazar had ruled there, two of the Three Holy Magi[6] who brought offerings to Our Lord in Bethlehem. Northeast of those lands are the kingdoms of Georgia and Abkhazia,[7] and the people who live there are pious, upright Christians.[8] To the north of them are situated the kingdoms of Greece and Armenia, and the people populating them are also Christians. All those people who live in those kingdoms are Christians, but they are not equally good Christians. They differ from each other through all kinds of articles and points in their faith, as described below.

Each one of these kingdoms is just as powerful as the one ruled by the Sultan except that some are located next to water and deserts, apart from other natural barriers. About all these Christians who live in these lands, we must say that neither one believes in the same faith as the other. Some are called Latins, Syrians, Indians, Nubians, Armenians, Greeks, Georgians, Nestorians, Jacobites, Maronites,[9] Copts, Ethiopians, Maronians, and Soldinians.[10] All these groups of Christians who live there have all kinds of their own churches, but no one enters into the churches of the others.

Prester John

Prester John is a Christian and the lord over India and he wields more power and is stronger as a ruler than the emperor of Rome.[11] Insofar as he is the ruler of India, he has been identified as Prester John. And in all of his letters he writes that there would be no greater and more noble title than that of a priest. This is so because through a priest's power both heaven and hell are unlocked and locked, and when a priest lifts his arms up, then all the emperors and kings fall down on their knees. Furthermore, the most noble city in India is called Seuwa,[12] the site of the priest's residence. It might be too tedious to describe at length how splendid and beautiful are his palaces and houses, decorated with gold and gems. This is no wonder since people buy and sell all things with the help of paper money.[13] They make use of gold and silver for jewelry and rings. In all the countries of India and Tatary, they buy and sell everything with small pieces of papyrus that are signed and correspond in value with gold. When a person owns too many of those signed pieces that are no longer valid or cannot be used any more, they [the bankers, or government officials?] give him new bills as a replacement for the old, and this without raising any charges or complaints.[14] All the people who live in India are Christians, and they have a patriarch called Thomas whom they all obey,[15] just as we obey the pope in Rome. When the bishop anoints priests, he burns them with a sharp red-hot iron from the forehead down to the nose, causing a wound and a cut that will be a sign for the rest of their lives. They have this practice as a symbol indicating that the Holy Ghost entered the Apostles with fire.

All their monks follow the rules of the Order of Saint Anthony[16] and Saint Macarius [of Egypt],[17] wearing long rough and wide gowns of fur and grey coats, and small hoods that are open in the front.

The knights in India behave very properly in all matters; they hunt animals and enjoy falconry.[18] They wear very elegant clothing, have golden belts, and use precious bows and arrows when they ride out to the open fields, not experiencing any discomfort, only joy and happiness.

The women and maidens in India are all ugly and brown-skinned,[19] and this irrespective of the fact that they wear rich and delightful clothing along with jewels such as gold and gems – a topic that would certainly deserve to be discussed at length. Their clothes are finely woven out of golden thread and cut in the style of women's dresses. Underneath, they wear undergarments of bleached white fabric impregnated with so much perfume of noble herbs that one can smell them in the streets whether they walk or ride on a horse. Their dresses are richly embroidered with pearls and precious stones, along with other precious objects typical of women. I would have to say much more about how beautiful they are.[20]

Translation

All the priests in India, when they get ready for Mass,[21] along with the deacons and sub-deacons approach the altar from three directions to symbolize that the Three Holy Magi had come from three directions and three countries to go to Bethlehem to the manger. The people in India are much smaller in size than other people and use a childish language.[22] They cannot tolerate freezing temperatures, and whenever they want to travel beyond their country, they wear long rough coats fashioned from furs of particularly noble animals. They then wear them in foreign countries, and the smaller they are, the more often they do this.

The country of India consists of islands[23] connected by bridges but divided by large bodies of water. The monks and the merchants who used to travel there say that the people who live closest to Paradise are all deaf from birth. They are all wise merchants, and all their selling and buying is done by means of signs. They operate with those just like a language. They are born deaf as a result of the terror of the firmament which moves very fast; they say that it rotates as fast as a mill stone. They also note that the sun rises in the morning with such a horrible noise that no human being can bear it who is not used to it.

They also say that there are many large swamps in which such large quantities of reed grass and cattails grow that they build their houses and ships with them.[24]

On other islands, there grow such good plants,[25] the best in the world, but there are many evil and large reptiles and snakes;[26] and without those, these good plants would be much more widespread than they are now.

Further, there are many islands on which you can find gold and silver, which the people deliver to Prester John. In the southeast of India, the people living there are not more than a foot tall, and the friars[27] and merchants buy them and sell them to the kings and lords, who buy them irrespective of the high price. These little people eat nothing but hemp seeds in their country, and the merchants have to bring those with them because if those dwarves cannot eat them, they die immediately. They do not speak a language that people can understand because they squeal like mice. Their country lies the closest to Paradise. The merchants say that the people in that country and in neighboring countries suffer badly from cranes [because they attack them (?)].

Next to that country, there is another island. The people who live there do not have a head, but their eyes and mouths are located in their chest.[28]

In that country there are yet other islands. The people who live there have large ears which are thin and of such a size that they can cover their bodies with them.

Moreover, in India, there are other islands where the people who live there have heads like dogs. In that country, the good Apostle Saint Thomas was killed.[29]

In another country, there are people who have only one foot which is as thin as a foot of a goose [claw], and so wide that they can protect themselves with it from the sun and the rain, and even from wild animals. Those people are very fast and good shooters [equipped with bow and arrows].

In India, there are other islands populated by people whose mouths are so small that they imbibe all their nourishment with straws. There are representatives of all those [monstrous] people mentioned above at all of the courts of princes and lords in other countries. There are very rich merchants, and they wear furs from all kinds of animals, and they are mostly bad Christians, and they accept the faith as practiced by the lords at whose court they live.[30] Those people believe that we are very strange, just as we regard them as outlandish.

Leaving all those people behind, you get to the Red Sea; there flows a river which empties into the Paradise river, which in turn flows through Egypt to Alexandria.[31] From there, all commerce is directed toward India again, where the Sultan pays his tribute to Prester John because the latter is the ruler over all those countries described above. I could also address many other foreign people, animals, birds, and riches to be found in Prester John's country (there would be much more to say about all that).

The kingdom of Nubia,[32] where Melchior, who brought gold as an offering to Our Lord, ruled as a king,[33] is also located in the southeast, where Prester John rules. The people in all those countries are called Nubians; they are the best Christians, and they speak Chaldean and also write Chaldean.[34] They enjoy the highest respect among all other Christians in the countries beyond the sea ["Outremer"]. They control their own churchyards and churches everywhere, like the Frisians in Aachen.[35] In honor of King Melchior, from whose country they and all their priests originate, they wear, when they want to celebrate Mass, a crown made out of gold or silver on their heads, depending on their personal wealth.[36] They do that as a symbol of the fact that the Three Holy Magi brought offerings to Our Lord while wearing crowns.

Prester John is also the lord over the country of Tharis, which had been ruled by King Caspar. The people there are black Moors[37] and there they are called Soldinians, and they speak their own language.[38] The people in that country, or wherever they might be living, make and paint Our Lord and Our Lady Virgin and all saints in black and the devil in white because they themselves are black and bad Christians. For that reason, they do not receive that much respect from other Christians, like the people in the country of Nubia and the bishops and priests living there. When they say Mass, they hold a golden star above the altar as a sign of the star that led the Three Holy Magi from their country to Bethlehem and to the manger.

Prester John is the lord over four kingdoms where bad Christians live everywhere. They are called in that land Nestorians, whom Pope Leo and many other saints had converted. But they fell back to their wrong faith, and therefore God has strictly divided them. They are disregarded [or valued little] by the heathens [Saracens/Muslims][39] and the Christians, and they live under the rule of Prester John and the emperor of the Tatars [Mongols]. They exist together without any government and without paying taxes like the Jews; after only a few years, they have lost their entire land, so that they do not have their own king or lord. But they live under different lords and they inhabit a particular island called Egrisula.[40]

Caspar, one of the Three Holy Magi [Three Holy Kings], was born there, and Saint Helena gave the corpse of the Apostle Saint Thomas for his corpse, when she called together the Three Holy Magi. To the present day, the body of Saint Thomas still rests on that island called Egrisula. But there is no truth to all those miracle stories people talk about. But it is probably true that he had been interred in a different country because now he is buried alongside plain heretics who did not know any [religious] order/rule like other people who are put to rest anywhere on the other islands of the two Magi.

In many countries there are bad Christians who do not have their own country or their own lord, as you can read below. They live with other people in those lands.

First, there are those bad Christians who are called Jacobites who do not believe in the Holy Trinity, and therefore they bless themselves with one finger, and their priests, deacons, and sub-deacons stand together around the altar and receive as a group the Holy Sacrament according to their custom, and they do that in memory of the Three Holy Magi who in the past had brought offerings to Our Lord in Bethlehem.[41]

Moreover, in that country there are other bad Christians, who are called Copts. They live mostly in Egypt and have a special book [gospel] which they call the Secrets of Saint Peter, which they use in their Masses as Epistles, and they worship the Gospel written by Nicodemus. They have their own bishops and priests who dedicate their Masses throughout the year to the Three Holy Magi.

Further, in that country there are yet other bad Christians who are called Maronites. They clean and maintain their churches extremely well, especially when they catch sight of a spider or a worm therein, or when the sun shines through a hole. And their priests certainly separate the men from the women, whether they like it or not. Their priest deacons have their married wives, and they offer Mass on one day dedicated to Saint Thomas and the other day to the Three Holy Magi, except on *Kirchweih*[42] or Easter.

Further, other bad Christians live in that country, called Ysinians,[43] and when they baptize their children and make them into Christians, the priest burns a cross into their forehead with an iron so that they can be well recognized as the good Christians they want to be. They mostly live in Egypt and believe that they need to grow in numbers so that they can march toward Babylon where the Sultan resides. Each one of them would then carry a rock or a piece of limestone with him, leaving nothing behind.[44]

In the year 1341 A.D. [C.E.], the Christians in that country were slain, just as when the Jews died in our lands.[45] Then the Egyptians expelled the Ysinians because they thought that their numbers had grown too much. Then the Sultan said that hardly a day would pass during which people would not bring a thousand cartloads of stones to his construction site. Each stone was cut into so many pieces, more than the number of children born from the Ysinians per day. Thus, he calmed the people, easing their fear that they might be slain.

When those preachers want to read Mass and then finish with it, then they bless the people, wishing that God protect them and guide them in all things here on earth as He guided the Three Holy Magi and led them without any harm and suffering to His manger.

There also live other evil Christians in that land, the pagan Maronians.[46] Whatever works or projects they take on, they pronounce that they have embarked on them in the name of God and the Three Holy Magi.

There are many other bad Christians, mostly near Antioch, who are generally called Nicolaitans and firmly believe that neither a man nor a woman, neither a servant nor a maid, can do penance to God for the sin of others when one person begs the other to commit unchastity and then denies him that.[47] But among those people, no one is so poor that cannot give three alms of bread per day in honor of God and the Three Holy Magi.[48]

The Kingdom of Georgia

The kingdom of Georgia and the kingdom of Abcas [Azerbaijan] are situated in the northern parts of the Orient.[49] The people who live there are also Christians, and they demonstrate great skill with weapons. The first people are the Georgians, who are very strong and have their own language. They ride across the lands in great groups, just as the Frisians do.[50] They carry a banner or a flag with them wherever they go upon which Saint George is depicted, after whom they call themselves Georgians. They travel across the lands of the Sultan and all of their lords without paying any tariff, free and without any harassment because this makes them more attractive to the Muslims who live in Mecca, in their countries, and in the desert. The monks and the priests of that country follow the rules of Saint Anthony and Saint Macarius,[51] and they are also the monks who live at Saint Catherine on Mount Sinai. Wherever those people travel, they sing and read about the Three Holy Magi, begging them to lead them across the mountains and deserts. That country is a large kingdom and is called Upper Georgia.

The kingdom of Abcas [Azerbaijan][52] is called Lower Georgia. In the old days, it was called Armenia, and the country mostly consists of high mountains. In this country there is the mountain upon which rests Noah's ark. But, because of the snow, no one can climb up there. You can see the snow also on other high mountains. You cannot see anything anymore of the ark on the mountain since there is nothing left apart from a tree that had burned a long time ago. The people who live in that land say that it dates from the time of the ark.[53]

In Georgia, there is yet another country which the people there call *Heynissen*.[54] It is five miles in length and width. Around that country and inside, there is a thick fog and darkness up to the sky, so you cannot see the sun at noon when it passes across the country.[55] People live around that fog and also in the middle of it, so they can hear horses neighing and roosters crowing. I have never heard that anyone has ever entered the fog in which those people live, or that anyone who lives in that fog has ever come out to the people on the outside. But there is nothing between both worlds that would prevent anyone from entering that foggy country. People live around the fog because there are many pastures. One can read that Mohammed conquered the entire country with his might, so all the Christians fled into the mountains. The Muslims followed them accompanied by their wives and children, and with all their property because it is their custom to move with military might wherever they want to settle. There they pushed the Christians to a location in the mountains. And when the Christians realized that they could not escape, they appealed to God, to Saint George, and the Three Holy Magi, who at that time were in Constantinople, to rescue them from the Muslims. Then that ominous fog rose up to the sky around all the sites where the Muslims camped,[56] so that from that time on no person has ever come out of it or has entered it, even until today.[57]

Accordingly, the people are called Georgians; they are very brave and powerful people who move around in large groups like the Frisians. Wherever they travel, they carry with them a banner or a flag upon which are depicted the Three Holy Magi. They commemorate with great festivities the day and the time when they had been rescued in that way, wherever

Der Niederrheinische Orientbericht, c.1350

they might be. These two kings of Georgia wield much more power than the Sultan. But the Sultan and the Muslims live with them in peace and wisdom. Wherever the Georgians move or travel, they sing songs about their rescue from the Muslims.

The Kingdom of the Greeks

The kingdom of the Greeks extended for a distance of 200 days of travel in length and width.[58] It comprised the countries of Babylon, Asia, Egypt, Turbia, Armenia, Cilicia, Achaia, and many other countries. Those the Greeks have lost since the time when they resisted the See of Rome [the papacy] and turned away in their faith. Now, the emperor of Constantinople lives there, and they also have a patriarch whom they obey as we do with the pope. The chapters, articles, and points through which they differ from us are as follows:

First, they do not believe in purgatory, and they also do not believe that the Holy Ghost originates from the Father and the Son, but only from the Father. But now, as of a few years ago, at the time of Pope Innocent, they have returned to the proper faith and have submitted themselves to the See of Rome.[59]

Their priests have wives and sport long beards, and when they elect a bishop all the priests vote for him during the assembly, among themselves. Then his wife joins a convent, a place where he never comes to see her. But should she want to see him during the day or at night, she may come to visit him and sleep with him without anyone objecting to it.

The Greeks do not eat meat for a third of the entire year, but during the day they eat as often as it pleases them.

In all those countries where they exert legal authority, they never execute anyone whatever crime he might have committed.[60] Instead, they cut off his beard, which is regarded there as shameful as when they cut off an ear here [in Germany]. Whatever he might have stolen, he must then return to the value of seven times the original, or he spends a year and a day in prison.[61]

When someone kills another person, then they cut off his hands and feet and gouge out his eyes.

The Greeks' clothing is usually dark blue, and their coats are long and wide and have long wide sleeves. They do not wear hoods on their heads, but hats of black felt with wide brims.

The Greek women wear dresses of great value embroidered with gold and pearls. The normal clothing of the women in this country is white, sewn out of linen strips, and the maidens' dresses are long and wide smocks like albs.[62]

They keep their churches very clean. They are filled with the smell of incense during the entire day.

Their priests sing Mass three times per week in the morning. But on Thursday, they sing the Mass after Vespers as a reminder of the fact that Christ had prepared the holy Eucharist himself in the evening. When they sing or read Mass, then no one is allowed to stay close to the altar. Then the priest cuts an oblate from a simple slice of bread, and thereupon he blesses the bread, and hands it out to all the people. The main priest then places the oblate in a golden vessel and puts a golden star on top of it, which is bent, and covers it with a clean cloth, which all priests then carry on their heads in a dignified manner, with candles and with incense, all around the church. They do that as a symbol of how the star led the Three Holy Magi to the true God.

They pour wine and warm water into the chalice, and when they read the Gospels, the deacon shows the chalice to the people, and when the priest reaches the moment when the holiest prayer is spoken, he sings even more beautifully than before.

During the thirteen days, they perform all Masses in Latin in honor of the Three Holy Magi. In their own countries they have good bells in their churches, but when they live among other people [under the rule of other lords], they beat on a piece of wood like a drum, and with that they announce the specific time of the day. On festive days, they beat on a piece of iron with a wooden stick. They place that on their shoulders and hit it twice, which makes the iron ring.

No Greek person, whether rich or poor, wears trousers and shoes, but rather something like leggings that are, because of the heat of the sun, completely made out of red or black leather.

The kingdom of Armenia extends from Damascus to Antioch, and on the one side it borders the Sultan's country, and on the other it borders the Turks' country, and on the third side it shares a border with the Tatars, and on the fourth side it lies next to the sea. The people who live there are Christians and very skilled in weapons. Their priests observe all aspects of the Mass as we do, but they mix oil with wine and water in the chalice, and they eat meat on Easter Saturday, a practice that is long gone by now.

They worship a saint whom they venerate deeply, named Saint Sergius.[63] They call out his name during the war; they observe the fast so strictly for him that there is not one child who would consume any food in that evening. They observe the fast equally strictly during the season of Advent. And at the time of Pope John,[64] there was a king named Leo who had married the sister of the king of Cilicia.[65] He was a very brave and powerful man who had subjugated all of his neighbors, forcing them to pay a tribute. The Sultan liked him very much and enjoyed seeing him in his presence, granting him everything he wanted. At that time, King Philip of France called for a crusade through sermons and proclamations.[66] He declared that he wanted to conquer Jerusalem and the Holy Land, and he asked the king of Armenia to end his peaceful relationship with the Sultan. Then the latter promised the king of Armenia that he would grant him whatever he requested, and he offered him the land and the castle voluntarily which the king of Armenia was to wrestle from him with all his efforts. Thereupon the king of France urged him not to forget his Christian faith or to lose his courage, and he strongly urged him to break his peace with the Sultan. Subsequently, the Sultan took as his wives the best Turkish and Tatarian women who lived near Armenia, and those peoples to whom they belonged then helped the Sultan against the king of Armenia.

The other neighboring peoples, whom the king of Armenia had expelled, joined him, and they conquered the marvelous castle of Layas, for which there was no equal, and they also conquered more than four hundred castles down to a river which is as great as the Rhine, which was spanned by a very long bridge.[67] Located there is a monastery of the Premonstratensians, who defended themselves and destroyed that bridge; if that had not happened, they would have conquered all of Armenia and taken possession of it. But they destroyed the wonderful city of Tarsis, which was much bigger than Cologne but is still nothing but rubble even today.[68] In that city, the saintly Apostle Paul was born. In the market of that city a well rises from a stone, which is so strong and clear that all people there can draw enough water. The water from the well flows [in channels] through all streets, and it cleans all of the city on the inside and their houses. Not many Christians still live there, and you might break into laments about how beautiful and strongly fortified this city once was, and what beautiful churches and houses existed there.

The king of Armenia waged a very bitter war against the Sultan, but the king of France did not come to his aid when he lost his entire land and his people.

At the time of Pope Benedict,[69] the king of Armenia submitted to the Sultan's mercy so that the latter could take the entire land as his possession, and he also received three hundred thousand Florentine ducats as a tribute. Since the time when Christianity had lost Acre [1291] and Jerusalem or later, no other such great harm and damage at the hands of the Muslims had befallen it, and this at the time when the king of France had called for a crusade which then did not take place. Hence, the Christians in the country of the Muslims were slain and expelled just as had happened to the Jews over the outbreak of the Black Death.[70] Then the Christians begged God to impose considerable hardship on him,[71] because he had forgotten them. Immediately thereafter, the great war between the king of France and the king of England broke out.[72] Then the Christians in that country walked barefoot for a long time and wore a penitent's hairshirt as on Good

Friday, and they prayed to God to give the king of France his fair punishment because he had brought doom upon them. The people in Outremer believed that the defeat which the king of France experienced during the war had been imposed on him by God because of his sins.[73] Afterwards, the king of Armenia, with two dukes from *Kynck*,[74] again gained much power, and they caused considerably more harm to the Turks than before, but the Sultan did not intervene.

The country that is now called Armenia was called Cilicia in the Scriptures.[75] It is a very mountainous region with an amazing growth of fruit. The kings, princes, and lords present themselves very impressively, wearing belts and valuable quivers and arrows that they carry with them all the time, both the rich and the lesser-ranked people, when they ride on horseback or walk. When you spend time at their courts, the guests are not placed two at a time in front of a dish.[76] Instead, they bring in whole cooked and fried geese and sheep to the dinner table, from which they cut off pieces from the top to the bottom, and they do the same with other sorts of meat, whether venison or domestic animals. They bring huge pieces of it to the dinner table, where they cut equally large parts off it. But the ordinary people receive [cooked] roosters, doves, and other birds in dishes, as they do back home.

The women's clothing is very splendid, decorated with pearls. All the knights wear silk clothing which is long and wide, just as the Three Holy Magi wore when they brought their offerings to Our Lord.

In the country of Outremer, there are still other Christians who originated from the kingdom of Jerusalem who are called Surians [Syrians] because the country that used to be called India is now called Siria, so they are identified as Surians. In that country, they are also called belt-wearing Christians, because there are no other Christians wearing a belt. Those Christians happily spend Saint Barbara's evening in the country where they live, as we do here on Saint Martin's evening. Each person sends to the other some seed that he has to sow in his garden. Over the year, they have cleanly planted one seed next to the other in a cup.[77]

When they are at a legal court, they swear an oath on God and the Three Holy Magi as the people here do when they swear an oath on the saints.

The Mandopolians

In that country, there are other bad Christians, the Mandopolians,[78] who move around in large numbers with women and children and who never step into a house, neither in winter nor in summer. They move from village to village, undertaking some little jobs through which they earn an income, and their wives do not take their children into the houses, and they do not stay there longer than three days. If they were forced to stay there for more than three days, they would die. If they were forced to stay in a house for three days, they would also die [the author repeats himself here]. Those people speak their own language among themselves, which no one else can understand. But they comprehend the languages of other people very well. They never fight among themselves. However, when a woman finds her husband with another woman, or when a man finds his wife with another man, they do not become angry with each other; instead, if he can, the man tries to do the same with another woman.[79] So they move during summer and winter from one city to another,[80] and during both day and night they gather in large groups in the field or in front of a castle, making music with pipes and drums. Often, they steal what they eat and drink; when they come to a very large village, they perform a show to which everyone comes running [paying them a fee], but otherwise, they steal what they want to eat and drink.

Those people adapt to the local customs, wherever they go, whether they are Christians or Muslims, during their entire stay, during eating or drinking, or during the fasting season; they themselves have no lords or priests. Irrespective of what kind of Christians, their women come with their children, they let them be baptized accordingly, and when they are together with any Christians on Sundays, they go with them to their churches playing their pipes and beating their drums, and they celebrate Mass in honor of the Three Holy Magi so that God leads and protects them in their names, wherever they might travel across mountains or deserts.

Under whatever Christian order they suffer their death, they are buried according to their customs/faith.

Conflicts and Differences Between Muslims and Christians

The Muslims also worship the Three Holy Magi, whereas otherwise they gouge out the eyes and cut off the noses of all of the saints whose sculptures they find in those churches that they have taken from the Christians and that they have destroyed. But the sculptures/pictures of the Three Holy Magi they leave untouched.

The Persians are also heathens,[81] but they pray with the Christians in their churches, and they say that after the time when the Three Holy Magi had been led from the east to the west, the star had never been seen, which is called in their country the guiding star.

In the countries of Outremer, all people wear special badges so that one can easily recognize what people and what faith they belong to. Those badges are pieces of cloth [a scarf] that the people wrap around their heads as protection against the heat of the sun. For that reason, the Muslims wear a long, white cloth around their head, which is called Hamema; the Christians wear a long cloth around their head that is striped in blue, and the

Translation

Jews wear a long yellow cloth around their head, and the Samaritans a red cloth.

The Jews in the Holy Land

In the lands of Outremer, not only the Christians are separated from each other in matters of faith, but also the Jews; there live not only all kinds of Christians, but also all kinds of Jews, such as Samaritans, Sadducees, Essenes, and they all originate from Abraham and hate each other more fervently than the diverse Christians do.[82]

Further, Jews live in the kingdom of Jerusalem, and that country is called Judea, and for that reason they are called 'Judeans' in the Gospel and 'Jews' in German. They follow the Books of Moses, as all people know well, and they work in that land, producing particularly valuable fabric from which is made clothing called linen dresses; and they bleach cloth as is the custom in that land. They also work as moneylenders, but they are not allowed to accept weapons as pawns.

Jerusalem is five miles away from Samaria,[83] which is called the kingdom of Israel; Jerusalem is the name of the kingdom of Judea. Tribes that belong to that country elected their own king, Jeroboam, who made them worship golden calves, as you read in the Bible.[84] And because the kingdom belonged to Samaria, the Jews living there are called 'Samaritans.' They do not want to have anything in common with the Jews, and they hate them intensely; they eat pork to irk the other Jews.

Further, there are Jews in that land who are called Sadducees.[85] In part, they also observe the Scripture by Moses, but they do not believe, as the other Jews do, in the resurrection of the dead. There are not many of them, and yet they do not want to have anything to do with the Jews or the Samaritans.

Other bad Jews also live in that land, who are called 'Oseys.'[86] They persecute all people and do not let them live. The Oseys marry their own mothers and sisters so that their numbers grow; they choose a prelate whom they obey and for whom they are ready to die. If he demands from them that they kill someone, they do that on the spot, and when he requests that they go into water or a fire, they do that without any objection. The Christians and Muslims have suffered much harm from those people. For that reason, they are persecuted without mercy wherever they can be found, or wherever one learns about them.[87]

Faith and Customs of the Muslims[88]

In all the countries in Outremer, not only the faith of the Christians and the Jews differs among the various groups, but also the faith among the Muslims. Their ways of life are different in various ways, as I will describe

Der Niederrheinische Orientbericht, c.1350

below. There are Saracens, Tatars, Pagans, Turks, and Persians, then Ismaelites, Saracens, and Agartines.[89] The latter is an old name and people. The Jews and the Muslims descended from two brothers, Isaac and Ismael, and the Jews descended from Isaac and the Muslims from Ismael.

At the time of the Ismaelites,[90] the Saracens, that is, the Pagans, lived in the desert; they were crazy people, and they had neither a faith nor a law. In the year 852 after the birth of Our Lord, when Heraclius was emperor of Rome,[91] there was a pope in Rome called Pelagius, with whom there lived a monk called Sergius, to whom the pope did not give as much in gifts as the latter had expected.[92] Filled with great disappointment, he traveled across the sea and joined those crazy Pagans [Muslims]. He took as a servant a man who was a shepherd, who used to take care of camels; he was called Magomet[93]; he was a simple, mad person. Sergius promoted his own affairs so well that he gained the duchess of Arabia as his wife and made the people believe that he was a god. He preached to them so intensely about Magomet that he marched with the entire people and with all his power, to the chagrin of Christianity, to Antioch and fought there against the Christians.[94] The latter lost the war, and since then Magomet and the Muslims have stayed in that country until today. At that time, they still did not have a law or any faith. Then, Sergius wrote a new book about Magomet which is called *Qur'an*.[95] It contains information about their norms of living, and the book was written as a prophecy which no one can fully understand. He claims that we ought to regard Jesus, Mary's son, as a sacred prophet whom Magomet had, together with the Holy Ghost, placed in his mother's womb. It also specifies that just as God had sent him to destroy Moses's teachings, so He had sent him to destroy the faith that Jesus had preached and taught.[96]

The Muslims are asked to believe in God and Saint Michael, and His messenger, Machomet,[97] and they must follow the laws that God had sent them through His messenger Machomet. Those who observe those laws correctly, gain, so they believe, entry to Paradise that is filled with delights[98] and can choose from many beautiful women.

Jesus, Mary's son, is to be regarded as a saintly prophet because He is seated next to Machomet in Paradise and achieved many miracles in His life and after His death. He killed Jews out of hatred, and on the third [day] He rose from death, and Machomet then let Him enter Paradise to be with him. However, He would neither be the true God nor a human being; the person who would claim so in a sermon would have to be stoned; and for that reason, the Muslims leave the Christians' churches undamaged.

The Christians who live among the Muslims practice their faith without facing any obstacles, but no one is allowed to engage in a debate concerning the respective faiths. Also, no Christian is allowed to preach there publicly. Further, Machomet forbade the Muslims from eating any pork and drinking wine, or from eating any other animal, wild or domesticated, if they had not killed it themselves. They are required to observe a strict fast, though on Thursday evenings they certainly eat meat and whatever else they have, because the [Muezzin] calls from the tower[99] that they have permission to do so.

Moreover, the Muslims pray together seven times a day and at night, and the Muezzin calls from the towers that are built for that purpose, telling them to pray to God and His messenger Machomet; and they strictly observe the laws that God has sent them. At whatever location they might be individually, whether in the house or in the courtyard, or in the field, they kneel down, and that is the common custom in that land. Whether a person is riding on horseback or is walking on foot, each one has a little rug with him which they kneel upon and pray.[100] The rug is made in a quality such that each person can afford it, and the lords, knights, and ladies have the rug carried and brought to them.

Before they go to church,[101] they wash their entire body as thoroughly as they can, and they walk barefoot into the church; no one speaks a word, or greets anyone; instead, they pray in the direction of the south, just as the Christians pray toward the east.[102]

Their churches are not painted on the inside but are white; they store many books there and there is a stone column pointing toward the south where they turn for prayer.

When they want to confess, they fast until the evening and wash their body; then they climb up the nearest hill, and, fully repentant, they confess all their sins to God and Saint Michael and his messenger Machomet and their priests. They do not allow any Christian to enter their churches; a Christian who does so against their rule must become a Muslim, or they cut him into two pieces and pour the blood in the church and drag the bloody pieces through the church to re-consecrate it.

What we call a church, they call a mosque[103]; further, according to their law, they have seven wives.

It is a common custom to buy wives according to their age, and he who can afford to spend more gains more beautiful women.

A man can allow his wife to leave him when she so desires. Yet the person who accepts her can keep her, but then the [first] man cannot take her back, and they observe that custom very strictly.

Machomet instructs in his book that a man who has many wives and grants one of them to a religious man for the love of God will be given a hundred times more beautiful women in Paradise. That was confirmed [so it says] by Jesus, the great prophet, and therefore many people hand over their wives to religious men, just as here [in Europe] a man offers something in support of his soul. You can read in Machomet's books that Machomet and Sergius won, by means of those words, the best women from all countries.

Noble and powerful women have under their command a special group of servants and chambers, and none of these women share any community with the others, unless one of them specifically wants to come to the other; but the husband comes to her day or night, whenever he wants.

The poor Muslims who live in small houses sleep in all their clothing on mats; the wives and children rest there in their clothes, but they are very clean and white, and at night you hear all kinds of noises, crying and children's screaming. That, however, is so common that no one pays attention to it; a man there easily supports his wife and children because bread is cheap, and the people do not need much as food; they do not drink anything else but water.

When certain planets are in the right position, then the people in the towers call out at night that everyone ought to engender children since the constellation is propitious.

When a child who belongs to the servant class is born, it is circumcised like a Jew, and the day when it was born and circumcised, the child honors all his life once a year.[104]

In that country, they have a unique custom. When a man has impregnated his maidservant, then both, the maid and the child, are free.

Another custom is that the entire inheritance falls to the oldest child. If he is not competent, then the most intelligent and the best child inherits it all, and for that reason, all people prove to be superior in wisdom and virtues.

All people, men or women, who are caught in having committed a fraud, are cut into two, and no pleading can prevent that.

They consider it legitimate that when a Muslim or a Jew is caught with a Christian woman or a Christian man with a Muslim or a Jewish woman, the two are cut into two pieces.[105]

The Muslims place the corpses of their dead on the right side, and they bury them facing south, and they mourn them, following the Jewish custom, for forty days.

According to their own law, the Muslims have a highest dignitary whom they call a 'caliph,' to whom they are as obedient as we are to the pope. The caliph resided in Baghdad, but after the city had been conquered, the role of the caliph was abandoned.[106]

Moreover, the Muslims have bishops who are called kadi[107] and who exert much power in that country.[108] Among the Muslims, there are priests who are allowed to be only the sons of bishops. When it happens that a noble and powerful lord dies who leaves behind one or two wives who had loved him the most, the ones who had liked him the most and wanted to remain widows, those then go to the bishop and legally request from him that he should help them to conceive a child. He must not deny the woman's request [switch from plural to singular], he has to do that; or she demands forcefully that he goes to the grave of her husband along with her in order to create a child there. If the child turns out to be male, he is destined to become a priest, and if it is female, the bishop provides her with the social rank according to the mother's status. But the woman remains for the rest of her life a widow, and she cannot have another husband after the bishop.

Among the Muslims, you find monks, beghards,[109] beguines, religious women,[110] and oblates,[111] both men and women, who sustain themselves in many different ways through fraud, and this also in this land.[112]

Pilgrims visit the holy sites, and so also blind people with dogs to guide them, and they receive help so that they can travel to those sites like the other pilgrims.[113]

Further, there are particular hermits and recluses in the deserts who tend not to leave their cells and never talk with anyone, except once every year when their messengers travel to the lands [where the ordinary people live] and beg for alms. They claim that Machomet is constantly talking to them, and the [ordinary] Muslims consider them as very holy; many men and women rush there and ask that they include them in their prayers. Women, whose husbands have died, ask them about how they are coping in Paradise, whether they have there, by chance, much more beautiful women, and whether they might have the desire that they [the widows] follow them. When the time has then come for the answer on St. Lambert's Day,[114] then there are greater throngs of people there than here in Aachen.[115] In the evening, when all people have assembled, the hermits come from their cells, naked, flagellate themselves with whips, and make their entire body bleed, and all people follow them and scream just as the flagellants do. The hermits stay in the church at night, and when you ask the hermit the next morning what can be expected the next year, he then informs you about it, and people bring much [food]stuff and give it to the hermits.

There are many other charlatans, just as in our country, and there would be much to say and write about.

The Muslims commonly travel to the city of Mecca where Machomet [Mohamed, etc.] is buried. The city is located a twenty-five-day journey through the desert of Arabia away from Babylon,[116] where the Sultan resides. The travelers never see people or birds. The journey takes place every year in August during the great heat, traversing the burning sand. At that time, the camels lose their fleece and become hairless. The Muslims paint them, weave baskets with small branches, and hang those at the camels' sides. Those baskets carry everything they need during the journey. They travel in large groups through the desert because of the dangerous animals and reptiles, and because of the wild people who live in the deserts.[117] But of all the people who journey there, not even half of them return home safe because of the great heat and the lack of water. The dead lie there in great piles in the desert, and those people are then regarded as saints. At the time of Pope Benedict,[118] the Sultan ordered the setting up of very expensive cisterns in the desert wherever it was possible to do so.

When the Muslims arrive in Mecca, they perfunctorily make their confession[119] and then go to Machomet's temple to pray and to offer their sacrifice. When they want to return home again, each person throws a rock against the temple as a sign that they cast off all their sins and stone the devil. Thereupon they travel home filled with great joy and they are no longer concerned whether they die [on the way]. Those who have been to Mecca are praised by the entire family.

Further, they say that the temple in which Machomet is buried was the first house that was ever built by human hands. Adam used to live in that house, but you do not see anything of Machomet's corpse. A golden cloth hangs down from the vault, but no one knows what is in it. All the books by the Christians across the sea [in Europe] claim pigs had torn him apart at the end of his life.[120]

Many pilgrims who have been to the temple in Mecca are so devout that they subsequently no longer want to see any earthly things. There are some particular houses in which they are helped right away [to achieve that goal] so that they can never see anything anymore after that [they are being blinded], and those pilgrims then walk throughout the world with dogs and beg; they receive many donations.[121]

The Muslims, in the way of pilgrims, travel to the temple in Jerusalem which they call 'The Rock.'[122] When they want to get there, they say: "We want to travel to the Holy Rock in Jerusalem," because in the temple there is a small pile of stones encircled with iron grilles in an artistic fashion. Jacob slept next to that rock, and there was a ladder that led up to heaven on which angels climbed up and down,[123] and there Jacob struggled with the angel.[124] And on this very stone, Melchizedek sacrificed bread and wine.[125] On that stone, the angel stood when David angered Our Lord and put his sword back into the scabbard,[126] after he had struck down the people, and on this stone Our Lord was sacrificed in the temple,[127] and Simon took Him into his arms.[128] On that stone, the fire from heaven burned the sacrifice, and on that stone Our Lord sat and taught the Jews when Mary and Joseph had lost Him,[129] and on this stone Mary made her sacrifice. God has created so many miracles with this stone from time immemorial with His divinity and with His humanity, and this in the temple of which the Gospel tells us. And therefore the Muslims call it the temple "of the holy rock," and they

Translation

visit it coming from distant lands. The Jews also respect the temple greatly, but the Muslims now control the temple and do not let either Christians or Jews enter, and they themselves go barefoot into the temple, and they do that with great respect.

When a Christian wants to become a heathen [convert to Islam], no one forces him to do so. But when a pious man wants to become a Muslim, then they take him to their bishop whom they call "kadi." Then the bishop asks the Christian whether he wants to do that out of disappointment or out of monetary interest. Then he instructs him in all matters and invites him to learn more about the Muslim faith. When the Christian agrees, then no one can hold him back. The Muslims then place the Christian on a camel, and a servant runs next to the animal calling out that people should give their thanks to God and His prophet Mohammed because Christians, whatever distant lands they might come from, have joined their holy community. This is then [publicly] demonstrated by the Christian on the camel. Then they take the Christian to a cold bath in a house, wash him, and put new clothes on him, place a turban on his head, and treat him from then on as one of their own [as a heathen like them]. But he is then as little trusted as a Jew who has converted to Christianity. They never believe him and never offer him a drink of water, unless he has truly earned it. Further, Christian monks, canons, and priests are allowed to sing and read Mass in their churches as much as they like as long as they do not preach against the Muslims. The Jews who live among the Muslims are not as much esteemed as the Christians.

As to the merchandise which is transported via ships to the Sultan's land or is brought in under the Muslims' control, this cannot be sold until the merchants have first written to the Sultan about their goods. Whatever he then fancies, they have to send it to him and sell the other items on the market. But the merchants' costs and efforts are well compensated, and the merchants ride around in splendid clothing and with amazing jewelry. However, the authorities strictly ensure that no one can leave the country without official permission, about which I could say a lot more. Further, when a king sends his messengers (diplomats) to the Sultan, or when a mighty merchant arrives, the Sultan's officers welcome him with the gift of a beautiful horse and receive him very honorably, whereupon they accompany him in a dignified manner to the Sultan. A servant then runs next to him, shouting out that people ought to love God and Mohammed because they have such a worthy lord to whom mighty Christian kings send their ambassadors and who is visited by such mighty princes. The Christians must not offer wine for sale in the cities, although grapes are allowed for sale because they are small and yellow.

Moreover, there are very clean taverns in which they sell good water just as they sell good wine in our country. He who has the best water is visited by the most people. In the taverns, there stand silver vessels filled with water from which water flows out of small silver faucets. The vessels hang on a hook; the floor of the tavern is strewn with all kinds of greenery, upon which the Muslims place themselves, while singing and frolicking. There they offer many strawberries during the summer and winter, and their songs deal with bubbling springs like our songs deal with love, and then they order splendid food. Bad taverns are inappropriate for the serving of water, and if someone is trying to start a quarrel, then the other person orders him in the name of the Sultan to keep the peace. Thereupon no one is allowed to say one more word, otherwise he would have committed a grave crime.

All guest houses in that country are certainly pleasant, but there is no quietude. You get good food and drink there, and the lords have to bring their bedding and utensils with them as people walk and ride more during the night because of the great heat of the sun.[130]

The common clothes in that country consist of white fabric, very clean and long, extending down to the feet, and these robes are wide and have long, wide sleeves down to the hands. But the noble lords and knights wear such long wide clothing interwoven on the top with golden strips, studded with valuable gems, and the women's clothing is fabricated out of precious silk, with golden fabric. They paint their fingernails red. They have only one braid on the head which they twist very elegantly; they tie a cloth in front of their mouths and place a veil on their forehead, which is extraordinarily valuable. One does not see anything of their face except for the eyes.

All people who live in the cities are very wise and wealthy merchants, and they always give alms to the poor Christians and Muslims.

The Christians and the Muslims who live in the cities tolerate each other very well, and no one gets into a quarrel because of his faith because their judicial system [the legal court] is very harsh and punitive.[131]

The ordinary people who live in the villages also guard their affairs very well, but they are very limited and ignorant, and they do nothing else but tell what they have heard and have learned from their predecessors, because they have neither preachers nor priests, and wherever they go they clasp their hands together behind their backs.

In the year 1341 after the birth of Our Lord [A.D. = C.E.], the great dying began among the Muslims, but no Christians died; instead, only the Muslims and the Turks died.[132] Then the Muslims and the Turks decided among themselves that they wanted to become Christians in order to avoid dying. But then the Christians also began to die, and then the servants of the Sultan of India arrived and reported that the dying in India had lasted for three years and that not even a third of the people there had stayed alive. Having learned that, the Muslims and the Turks remained what they were.[133] And then about a thousand people died where at first only one had died. There would be much more to say about other cities and customs of the Muslims. All noble lords and members of monasteries have reported about them.[134]

The Sultan's Rule

The one individual among those Muslims who is their ruler is called their melek[135] and in other countries Sultan, and he resides in Babylon,[136] just as we talk about Rome where the pope lives, and he governs the country of Egypt, the country of Suria,[137] and the countries of Syria, Arabia, Philistia,[138] and Galilee, and all the cities located there.

Further, the Sultan rules over the king of Damascus and the king of Gaza, who is not entitled to an inheritance; instead, the Sultan appoints as the king of Gaza whomever he chooses. The same year when Acre was conquered [1291], the Sultan died who had conquered it; he was called Melek and Sapheraff.[139]

Then the princes and lords elected another Sultan, the crudest person whom they could find, and this with the purpose of getting some entertainment from that. The princes and lords coaxed him to support their side, and each one wanted to be his greatest favorite, which led to a steady decline of all countries; no more pilgrims arrived nor did any merchants come to the cities and villages. Therefore, the Sultan carried out, with the help of the ordinary people, legal trials and adjudicated cases for whoever asked for justice. The first thing for him was to have his son cut into two pieces, and thereupon all those lords and princes who had robbed the people. For that reason, the entire country turned into his loyal supporters so that he became the mightiest ruler who had ever been a Sultan.

This Sultan, in his physical appearance, was an ugly person, short and fat; he had a large head and a crooked nose, a short neck and large eyes; he was bent over and crooked, and lame so that his hand hung down to his knees. His name was Melek Mesor.[140] Although he appeared as a crude person on the outside, on the inside he was a most impressive person in terms of virtue and wisdom. His clothing did not correspond with the importance of his rule, consisting only of white silk, interwoven with golden strips and embellished with all kinds of gems. The turban and cloth that he wore around his head were surprisingly small, delicate, and made from thin silk and golden cloth. When he carried out negotiations[141] with lords sent to him, then his chamber, his weapons, and all paraphernalia placed around him were so impressively and luxuriously decorated with gold and gems that one could not even find words.

The prince or lord who was sent to him had to prostrate himself before him three times, and had to kiss the floor before his feet, and had to rest on his knees until he called upon him and told him to get up.

The Sultan's palace was situated in the city of Cairo[142] on top of a rocky hill, on the same spot where the pharaoh had lived when Moses and Aaron caused the miracles of which you can read in the Bible.

The Sultan ate and drank most modestly, and he slept little. When he got tired, either during the day or at night, he briefly laid down on a bed. When he presided over the court, he used to dine with his kings, princes, lords, bishops, prelates, and knights, and each person was seated according to his rank, and each one had his own special cooks. And his palace and his chamber were decorated with gold and silver, artistically vaulted, and decorated with frescoes telling the stories of how Joseph was sold [into slavery] and Jacob came to Egypt, and how Moses and Aaron created miracles there and led the people of Israel through the Red Sea.

On the outside of the chamber, the entire history of King Alexander was painted. The Sultan had all princes, lords, and knights dressed, and so also his son, who was, according to their customs, to succeed him as Sultan, with all kinds of golden clothing that had been produced and fetched specifically for that purpose, but they do not wear that clothing for long.

The Sultan Holding Court

The greatest assembly of the Sultan's court took place on St. Margaret's Day.[143] Princes, lords, knights, and merchants, Christians and Muslims, and all people got together at that assembly, and each person appeared dressed as splendidly and beautifully as he could. Many exotic and strange animals and birds from all over the world were brought there. One could see there many amazing, unusual people, animals, and birds, which were trained according to the respective local culture,[144] all in a particular art. You could find there many beautiful, luxurious pavilions set up by the lords, and also all kinds of unusual merchandise from the diverse countries in the world. Finally, there were many beautiful, precious stones that had been sent there to the Sultan.

When the princes and lords arrived at the court assembly in such a fashion, they also brought valuable silver and gold vessels and their own cooks. Those received as much meat from domesticated and wild animals as they wanted. They prepared it according to the wish and taste of each lord; and each cook had with him his own servants, dishes, and equipment, one better than the other. Countless people, each one wealthier and more dignified than the other, came to the court, and all princes and lords brought their dogs, falcons, leopards, and whatever wondrous people, birds, or animals they owned, along with the most extraordinary gems.

When that court assembly was set for Vespers,[145] for the entire day, Christians, Jews, and Muslims speaking all the languages of the world, arrived and sang, one after the other, a song of praise to God and to the Sultan, and they stood in front of the palace, where you could hear all kinds of amazing singing. When one group was singing, all the other people kept silent. Then the Sultan responded and thanked God that He had granted him this honor and begged them all to pray to God on his behalf.

When they went to dinner, musicians played tambourines and large and small trombones, of which they had so many that no one could speak to the others [due to the noise]. Thereupon the Sultan gloriously moved in, with all of his soldiers marching in front of him,[146] with coats of arms made out of gold.[147] When the Sultan and the other princes and lords were assembled in the hall, they found a long table in front of them upon which were placed gold and silver vessels. The princes and lords were given water to wash their hands.[148] Once the Sultan had sat down, he had a long chain of gems hanging around his neck, and each one of them had particular virtues and power in itself, and on his chest he wore an emerald, as broad as a hand, and all of his robe was covered with gems.

His table was set three steps higher than the other tables, and across from him there was another table upon which were placed deep golden vessels filled with water. On the table, there were glasses filled with the water that he wanted to drink. The king of Damascus was seated on one side of the Sultan and on the other was the king of Gaza, but they were placed one step lower than the Sultan. Between the two kings sat the eldest son who was to become the Sultan after him, and then the Muslim bishop. His clothing was dark blue, and he wore a grey cap [kufi] on his head. The princes and lords were seated next to his table. Then there were the elders who were present and sat opposite the table. Behind it were seated the foreign lords and legates who had been sent to the Sultan and were charged with visiting the court.[149] All people were arranged according to their rank. Seated at a table behind them were the Christians [clerics], knights, and merchants.[150]

The mightiest prince delivered the food to the Sultan in very large golden vessels, which he placed in front of the Sultan on the table. The latter then pointed out what he wanted to eat; then they took the dishes again and placed them on another table. The prince then cut the food that he desired to eat and had pointed out to him into small pieces, and placed it on a piece of bread, and the bread itself on a small golden plate. The Sultan took off the meat that had been brought to him and threw the rest back onto the golden plate. The one who had brought the food also served him. What was left on the dish, the others ate who stood near the table and served him.[151]

The other kings, princes, lords, bishops, knights, and servants who sat on the side went to their own kitchens with very beautiful and valuable dishes and fetched everything that had been prepared for them, and this all in good order and in a completely relaxed manner.[152]

The only kind of drink was pure cold water, but it was very good and healthy, and they drank it from very delightful cups in very diverse forms which everyone had brought there. But the Sultan drank from a glass, which was very precious.[153]

In front of him, on the table, the Sultan had small dishes made out of green metal. Whatever they served him as food or drink was dipped first into the vessel, and if it contained poison, the vessel burst apart. Such vessels come from India, and the person who sells them is paid in heavy gold.

I could still talk much about other languages and of beautiful, noble gems that were placed on the tables.

When the first dish was brought out, there were master musicians who had trombones made out of gold which they played not more loudly than necessary but loud enough so that they could be heard in the entire hall. Then other master musicians from all the languages and countries arrived, and one could enjoy many delightful sounds and songs. All their instruments were made from silver or gold, decorated with precious gems. After the instrumental performance, men and women stepped up and sang songs from all the countries in the world and in all languages. Each one sang his or her song after the other. One could hear many great songs, and you could observe many marvelous gems worn by men and women from all countries.[154]

Once the dinner table had been removed,[155] people [acrobats] came who knew how to jump and fight, to perform and to dance, many times in a curious fashion. Thereafter the strangest people from India appeared, as you can read about them, who performed and sang, each according to his custom, and there were many amazing and strange people and many unusual vestments. That was followed by people with all the exotic, foreign animals as they exist here on earth, which then also displayed their skills as their masters had taught them to do.

Afterwards, all the princes, lords, and rich merchants stood up, one after the other, and brought in their masters with the falcons and dogs.[156] Those had very noble leashes and head cups and jesses.[157] They displayed them all to the Sultan who was pleased while inspecting them. Then they asked the Sultan whether he might desire one of them, and once he had selected a falcon, he gave the owner so much money for it that he was satisfied.

Once all matters were settled, the Sultan asked all of them who were sitting there about their lives, and their wives, and then he was very joyous and sociable with all, and they also asked the same of the Sultan, and each one sat down with them who wanted to ask something. Once that was finished, the servants brought many precious and different herbs in valuable dishes, and then the Sultan got up and asked them to pray to God that they could get together the next time as good friends. Then each one rode back wherever he wanted to go. The court assembly lasted eight days, during which one could talk with the Sultan about one's concerns.

The Sultan's Wives

The Sultan has more than 300 wives, and even more unmarried women from all countries.[158] They all live each in their own chamber, according to her rank, and how much he likes her.[159] They also have command over servants, and no one ever saw those women with his own eyes, except when there was a court assembly. Here they sat together with other women who belonged to them,[160] in front of their windows, and the princes and lords who attended the court assembly brought all their wives with them in litters or palanquins.[161] When those women reached the court, they exposed their faces and showed off their necklaces and their precious objects made out of gold and jewels in front of all, as well and as beautifully as they could. When the ladies went to dinner, they all sat on golden pillows placed on the floor,[162] which was entirely and beautifully covered with all kinds of cloth. The tables set up there, at which the women ate, were two feet above the floor. Waiters served them very delicious food, and all the women had brought with them precious drinking vessels and their cupbearers, irrespective of the fact that there were more than enough of them in the palace.

The women, however, who belonged to the Sultan did not sit there on the floor; instead, they were seated so high that they could look down on all the people. They were served by the most noble and best people. All that appeared as if they were worshipping an idol, as their service rituals made it look to be that way to an outside observer. And every one of the Sultan's wives received, together with their maids, that kind of service, each according to her rank. All were adorned and covered with rare gems, of which one could say much.

The Sultan's Wedding

And in the year 1348 after the birth of Our Lord, on St. Stephen's feast day,[163] the Sultan married his best woman,[164] who was the daughter of the king of Damascus. The festivals held there at the court were so extensive that there was no wheat in the entire country for a long time since so much had been burned.[165]

There all women walked with their heads uncovered, bedecked with their jewels as well as each could do, each more splendid than the others. Everyone in the country had to attend, Christians, Jews, Muslims, merchants, pilgrims, monks and friars, and everyone had to dance behind the city. For that purpose, everyone had put on their best clothing; the court festivals lasted for a month, and when the bride was led from one palace to another, all streets were covered on each side with golden cloths. Kings walked in front of the bride, leading her horse, and all the lords and princes walked on foot in front of her. I would have to add much about the splendor of the bride's and the horse's decoration. The bride was followed by all the women, all wonderfully decked with their rich jewelry; they were followed by all kinds of people, with different languages, dressed in their elegant clothing. There was much dancing, and one could observe acrobatic performances. There was such a throng that no one could keep a distance from the others, especially in front of the bride. No one could speak to each other because of the noise, and the air in the street[166] was filled with the smoke of precious herbs.

Then followed the Sultan, who wore on his head a wreath of laurels. Whatever church they reached, whether it was one of the Christians, Muslims, or Jews, there the priests and monks stood on the outside, wearing their belts, and they sang, and when the Sultan and the bride reached the priests, they took off the wreaths from their heads and bowed before God and the priests, and all the various people's groups held their own court assembly, and each person was treated respectfully according to his customs.

Holding Court and Public Display

After the Sultan had carried out his court festival in this way, he demanded on the spot exact accounting of all people who had been entrusted with an office in any way. When there was no court assembly, then they gave the meat of wild and domestic animals to the Sultan's wives and their maids, whereas they gave a month's salary to the other court servants.

When the princes and lords from abroad came to the court assembly, they wore shoes with golden soles, and when they got off their horses, then the servants put other shoes made from leather on them, and the golden shoes were carried behind them. Their robes were wide and long, made of gold-threaded cloth; the entire set of bridles and bits of their horses consisted of gold, and on both sides of the horses, at the front of the saddles, they had bags hanging down which were made out of nets consisting of gold. They carried the best of their gold and gems in those bags.

The mercenary foot soldiers stay in the palace all the time, by day and by night, always in a group with their banner.[167]

The mercenary soldiers on horseback ride to the palace every morning and spend a great deal of time there until the Sultan wants to go to eat. Then they ride away and return at the time of Vespers; and when the Sultan wants

Translation

to ride on horseback, then he does it in the early morning before dawn or in the evening after Compline.[168]

Twice a year, the Sultan had the custom of going on a special trip.[169] This was in March and after August when the cranes and other birds tend to migrate.[170] He orders that the field along the river, which is called the Nile and flows through Egypt, at a length of two or three miles, be plowed and seeded, and when the fruits of the field are ripe, the cranes stay on them, whereas the other birds fly up in the air. Then the Sultan invited all the lords, princes, and knights who own falcons to come together at the same time to join him, and when the Sultan went for a ride in the morning, then all those people and the soldiers left the city. All houses remained locked until the Sultan had returned. The soldiers, both on horse and on foot, stood there with their weapons and with their drawn swords on both sides of the street. Then the Sultan passed through with his elephants, upon which they had placed small towers held together with thin branches. The first elephant and its tower were covered with yellow, and the second elephant with black cloths of silk. Then followed two elephants that were tied together with iron chains, shrouded with red cloth of silk. Between their towers there was a litter which made it possible to walk from one tower to the other. And the litter was made like a grille and was all open, completely decked on the inside with gold and silver. The ceiling consisted entirely of gold. The Sultan sat in the litter with his most favorite son, his falcons and other birds, and so many dogs specially trained for hunting with birds of prey. Above the elephant flew his banner, which was red, and next to the banner his superior mercenaries walked with many beautiful weapons made out of gold and with unsheathed swords. They were followed on horseback by all princes, lords, and dignitaries, and when the Sultan came out of the city, all mercenaries formed long chains on both sides of the passage. He then greeted everyone, one after the other, by his name, and his son did the same on the other side.[171] Whoever was riding next to him, followed him, and the others stayed behind. And when the Sultan was with the people, then all those on foot and on horseback split up[172] and one group then rode ahead and the other group behind, and a part was on both sides, and all camped around the city in which the Sultan wanted to stay, for two or three miles, that is, around the entire city and the villages because there were more than 100,000 horses, not counting other mercenaries and foot soldiers. Nevertheless, it caused fewer problems to provision all the horses and people than the 1000 armed men, and this also applied to the entire population resting there.

There was a custom: when a man stayed in a house for a year, then he made a mark there so that in the following year no one would enter the house other than he who had written the mark, except when he agreed to it. No one suffered from any shortage because the entire country had to bring food and fodder, or what else was needed, on mules and camels and donkeys all day and night. All people [soldiers] and horses received enough, but no one was allowed to go or ride where the Sultan was without the permission of his superior. But at night, each one had to return to his banner,[173] and when the Sultan and the people separated from each other, it was just as if the entire world had assembled there, and when the sun shone on the litter, one could see that from very far away.

Once the Sultan had reached the place where he had wanted to go, the servants removed the towers from the elephants and placed them around the Sultan's pavilion and tied them to each other and secured the place with wooden boards. Then all the lords, princes, and knights pitched their tents in a circle around that because all people had pavilions, each according to his wealth. All that looked as if a large city were situated there. All the falconers and hunters had their special place around the Sultan's pavilion. When the Sultan wanted to see the falcons fly, that is, where the fruit of the fields was growing, he did that very early in the morning. Then the Sultan rode with his best falcon to one end of the field, and the other princes and lords rode with their own falcons wherever they wanted to go. When they let the falcons fly, no one could hear a word because of the shouting of the falconers.[174] Around noon, when the Sultan returned to his pavilion, all the princes placed there what they had hunted with the help of their falcons. Then the Sultan inspected all of the falcons, asked for their names, and greeted all falconers by their names, and when all the cranes and birds joined together, no person had ever seen so many birds and cranes in one flock. Then each person took his own birds and cranes [which they had hunted] and ate them in the company of the Sultan, and each one talked about his falcon.

Once that was done, they rode with their eagles and other birds which were trained for that, to a site for fishing. There they set deep nets useful for that purpose into the river Nile which flows through Egypt, and then they let the sea eagles fly.[175] At the same time, the masters went with boats between the nets in the river, called the birds, and attracted them to larger fish in the water, and the birds dived quickly behind them. Thus, all the other fish fled into the net, and in this way they caught more fish in the entire river than all the people could consume. One could discover many rare fish, and when all that was completed the Sultan hunted wild asses that stayed in front of the dogs like pigs and jumped over them and the ropes [placed there], which was entertaining to watch, and then they hunted large game, of which they hunted much so that all people had enough to eat.

Translation

After all that had been completed, they returned to the fields where the cranes and other birds had assembled again. The people [courtiers] caught birds and cranes, let them live, and rode one or two miles up and down, and then they let the gyrfalcons fly.[176] Once those had caught enough birds, they returned to the hunters, landing on their fists, but when one of the falcons wanted to fly away [and escape], the Sultan and his masters called first. All masters knew that call well, and this call traveled in one hour for two or three miles from one person to another. Thereby all the falconers became aware of the gyrfalcon, and wherever it flew the falconers sent their living cranes that they had kept ready for that purpose. The escaped gyrfalcon got so tired by being occupied with those that the masters could catch it again. That made them all very happy, but when the falcon spread its tail feathers far apart while flying in the air, they were very unhappy.[177] When that happened, no one was allowed to return home until they had caught that falcon again. The one person, however, who brought it back, was richly rewarded for his efforts.

When the Sultan wanted to ride home again, no one dared to quarrel with anyone, and he who might have done that would have committed an egregious misdeed.[178]

When the Sultan returned home, all the mercenaries walked and rode with him, and all people who had stayed behind in the city came out to greet him.

Later, when he fancied a ride into the countryside, the young people had to race in front of him and strike the ball in a competition while seated on horseback. They had crooked sticks for that purpose; when the ball fell on the ground, they hit it with the stick up in the air; the one who let the ball drop to the ground had lost.[179]

Another group of people had to jump through a wooden ring that was hung up in the air; whoever touched the ring had lost.

A third group set up target shields and shot onto them in a competition against each other.

He [the Sultan] owns horses that are of the size comparable to horses worth twelve guilders. They are called Arabians and run so fast that you can hunt down deer and does with them. And when a race rider rides on them in front of all people, he jumps over the marks that have been set for that purpose. But he who does not know how to control those horses [rein them in] loses his mind as soon as he is sitting on the horse [gets terribly frightened or discombobulated].

Further, there were other masters who constructed artistic [artificial] dragons [kites] that soared up into the air, held by a string, just as they wanted, both high and low.

When the Sultan wanted to ride out, the rich merchants displayed their goods in the open field. You could find many beautiful gemstones, and what the Sultan desired to have, they took to him at the palace. Only then did the others purchase what they wanted. When the merchants wanted to return home and said goodbye to the Sultan, each one received a letter issued for an official at the place where they wanted to go. Then they named the price for the wares that the Sultan had accepted from them, and the courtiers paid them in the form of the Sultan's gold, spices, sugar, cotton, or silk cloths, or whatever was valuable in that country, or whatever the merchants wanted to buy for themselves. When the official did not have it, then they purchased whatever they wanted, and the official granted that to them. But the Sultan never paid for falcons or trading goods with money; instead, he always exchanged one good for another, and he treated the merchants in such a way that they thanked him.

The Sultan enjoyed building, and he participated in it [as an architect] and wanted to be a master in that skill. Castles that he had built previously he later had torn down again. The people who had been taken prisoner in Acre and in Armenia had to do the construction work and had to carry stones and mortar. There were more than 6000 of them who were Christians: princes, lords, knights, and Templars, monks, and priests from many countries; all of them prisoners. They [the Muslims] treated them very well, and at night they all went to a large courtyard to sleep there. They all observed the resting time. But no one could gain his freedom, and they formed large groups among themselves when they assembled for the night. They were kept for a ransom, and however rich or noble they might have been they all had to work as much as the poor people; and they received a monthly salary for their food and clothing so that they had enough. Those who could not work were exempted from it, and each went to his house to eat, but at night they had to sleep together in the safe compound. But on Sundays or holy days they did not do that; they had their own beautiful church in which Saint Barbara is buried, and they had their own priests and let them, whether they were sick or healthy, guide them and bury them there in that land, and the Sultan also granted that the Jews, who were held prisoner, were allowed to observe their Sabbath, and he treated all prisoners very well, whether they were healthy or sick.

The Sultan owns a very beautiful library which contains the Bible, the Gospels, and the decretals,[180] and all the Christians' and the Jews' books, and chronicles, and those books had been translated from Latin into

Arabic. In particular, he [the Sultan] had ordered translations of books that deal with the law.

When the Sultan besieged a palace or a castle, then it was his custom that they [his servants] first set up a white pavilion and ask for negotiations.[181] When this was not accepted, he set up a yellow pavilion closer to the castle than the first one. At that point, one could still negotiate with him. But when that did not happen within a set time frame, he set up a red pavilion, and there were no more negotiations, and he was not willing to withdraw until he had fulfilled his will, or until he himself had been beaten and driven away. When he had conquered a castle, that served to increase his honor, and he left all things in that castle undisturbed.[182]

The Sultan observed peace with all his neighbors, unless he was forced to act differently.

He was always positively inclined toward pilgrims, monks,[183] and religious people.

Turmoil in the Sultan's Kingdom

Six years before his death,[184] the country began to rise up against him and there was a widespread rumor that he was a Christian. Together with the rulers of the [neighboring] countries, the king of Gaza and his own eldest son attacked and persecuted the Christians with utter brutality, wherever they lived, in villages or in cities, and the Sultan's son slew a Christian and the Sultan then had him executed after a legal court had pronounced the death penalty; he was cut into two pieces.[185]

The king of Gaza destroyed, to harm the Christians, a passage leading high up the mountain to the monastery where Our Lord fasted for forty days and forty nights,[186] and caused much harm to the Christians. Once the Sultan had put it about that the court had prosecuted his son and then had him executed, being cut into two pieces, the king of Gaza fled with his helpers into the desert so that no one knew where they had disappeared.

The Sultan had a servant with the name of Tenghes, who was a Turk and had so much courage and bravery that the Sultan gave him the daughter of the king of Damascus as his wife, and also the best women who existed in the country.[187] Tenghes became so powerful and rich that he had at all times 12,000 horses ready to ride and ruled over the entire country. Then he grew even worse [evil], while he had been good before, and he persecuted all Christians more viciously than all others had done, and he ordered that in his country no Christians would be allowed to ride on horses; instead, they had to resort to donkeys, and the non-Christians fully agreed with that.

At the same time, in the year 1343 after the birth of Our Lord, the war between the king of Spain and the queen of Sicily and Morocco, and the king of Granada broke out.[188] That queen visited the Sultan and asked for advice and support. She traveled across Barbary and gave the Sultan many precious, beautiful gems, more than had ever been handed over [as gifts] since the time of King Solomon. She also brought him [as gifts] three hundred splendid horses from Spain, all with golden blankets and bridles. When the queen had been there for a while, she traveled to Mecca where Magomed is buried. In the meantime, the Sultan ordered all the people from the entire country to assemble, and when the queen returned, men and women processed toward her, walking and riding on horseback in a most impressive fashion. To match that, the queen, her maids, and her people [knights] put on all their jewels as best as they could, and this in such a splendid manner that no person had ever witnessed before. They held a court that was more stunning than any other before. Then the Sultan displayed to her all his jewels and his wealth, and she stayed there for a long time with him and traveled from city to city.

When she wanted to return home, the Sultan gave her, her maids, and her servants so many precious things as had never been seen before. From all those gems, the queen did not take anything but a small rooster out of gold that Eraclius of Cosdras had won.[189] This was the rooster that Magomet had recaptured from Emperor Eraclius when the latter had lost the battle, and he took a ring and other precious objects from him which the Queen of Saba had dedicated to the temple in Jerusalem. This is the reason why the royal treasure of Egypt has stayed there until the present day. The queen had brought with her more than one hundred apostates,[190] who had been very good priests. But the Sultan did not want to deal with them, and he defeated them [in debates] with their own rules by means of a large number of books that they had composed against the holy faith.

The Sultan advised the queen to wage a war with the king of Spain and with the Christians. He denied her his assistance, and he predicted everything as it later became true. At that time, the king of Damascus was the highest advisor of the queen, and he hoped that she would take him as her husband, and she let him keep this illusion. There would be much to say about the great honor that he granted and demonstrated to her.

Persecution of Christians in Damascus

In the year 1341 after the birth of Our Lord, a street in Damascus burned down almost completely. Thereupon, the king announced that the Christians had done that, so the Muslims in Damascus slew all the Christians, men, women, the old and the young. All the streets turned bloody, and they killed the Christians as it happens to the Jews in our country.[191] Many Christians fled into the mountains and into the desert. The best [Muslim] officials caught the Christians and let them live, but the common people slew them all, and this misery lasted for a month. Subsequently, on the feast day of Saint Servatius,[192] the Sultan traveled to Damascus with all the Christians he could reach and ordered that the king of Damascus be fetched and tied onto a donkey. He took all of his treasure, which was so great that it could not be counted. He had the king dragged behind the city. Then he had him brought back, and he handed him over to the Christians of Babylon to do with him as they pleased,[193] and a merchant from Narbonne finally drowned him. The Sultan expelled the king's daughter and his wife, and also his servants; they found many letters with the king and his daughter that were aimed against the Sultan. For instance, a letter suggested that the wife should poison him. Then the Christians in that country sat down in honor of the feast day of Saint Petronilla,[194] as it otherwise happened during Easter.

The Muslims and the Turks

In the world of the Muslims there lived unique Pagans,[195] who observed neither the law nor the faith. Whatever they catch sight of in the morning, they pray to all day, although there is nothing to that object or animal. Those Pagans lived mostly in Damascus and were very intelligent and skillful masters in all crafts, but they have disappeared today because the Sultan did not want to have anyone living in the country who would not believe in God, who has created heaven, and the earth.

There are yet other Pagans who are called Turks and live in a country called Turkey, which they have conquered from the Christians and which extends from Damascus to Antioch and even up to Constantinople. It is a very large, beautiful, and good country with fruit and wheat, with cotton and willows, and there are many high mountains and many flat fields; there is much wood from the forests, and good things and good trade, but there are no large cities or villages in that country. And they do not have a ruler. But he who owns a castle owns all that he can control. There are also old houses and sheds situated in front of the castle, built out of stone and made out of arches, which makes it unnecessary for them to have rafters or beams. There are not many wells [of natural occurrence] in that country, but plenty of cisterns [artificially built]. Those are very clean and the water from them is very good. The language and clothing of the Turks are like those of the Muslims, and they follow their faith.

Even though Turks live in proximity to the Greeks, who are Christians, the male Turks probably marry a Christian woman, and a Turkish woman marries at times a Christian man. When they have children, then the son follows his father's faith, and the daughter the mother's faith. The greatest and best cities in Turkey are Antioch, Candelot, Satalia, Sichki, Schalbonnire, Altelot, and Saleff.[196] There were many splendid cities, villages, and monasteries in that country, but those have by now all disappeared and are abandoned.

Turks live in Antioch, but the city is destroyed to a large extent. The Turks pay a tribute to the Sultan because it belonged to him after he had conquered it from the Christians. It is a very beautiful city, wide and long, situated at the foot of a mountain upon which was located a very well fortified castle. The Sultan placed his Muslim soldiers in it. He had to besiege it for ten years before it was conquered. On the mountain, there were many wild animals that used to roam around. When the Christians lived there, they used to hunt the wild animals by chasing them into the city, where they could hunt them in the streets.

A very big river runs through the city and outside in which they [the Turks] could catch large fish. They used to place them in salt and exported them in large quantities to various countries. There is a gate that is still called 'Fishgate.' There is also a very long [fortified] bridge made out of stone, near where Geoffrey of Bouillon fought many fights.[197] He got into the city by crossing the bridge, once he had conquered the city. He besieged it with great difficulties for a whole year, as it is depicted in the palaces and courts back in the city. There he discovered under the soil the spear that pierced Our Lord when he hung on the cross, which the emperor now owns, as St. Andrew testifies.[198]

The city is half a mile in length and grows out from the churches of St. Peter and St. Paul. Its streets are very pleasant, and wide; there are many beautiful monasteries and churches. In the middle, there is an impressive cathedral, with St. Peter being its patron saint. Geoffrey was crowned there, and there is the throne upon which he was seated, and there are beautiful palaces and houses that are devastated now; and I could tell you much more about it.

The Turks own yet another city called Satalia,[199] surrounded by three rings of city walls and moats, built like three cities. In one quarter there live the Christians who celebrate Sunday; in the other quarter there live the Jews who celebrate Saturday. In the third quarter there live the Turks, who celebrate Friday. They have there a picture that Saint Luke painted of Our Lady. Through this picture, Our Lord created great miracles in that country, and outside the city there is a new city in which live the monks who perform a very impressive Mass. Very rich merchants live there, and that city belonged to the bishop of Orthosa.[200]

The Turks possess yet another city, called Ephesus since antiquity, but now called Altelot.[201] That city is located between two mountains, and in front of the city originates a river emerging directly out of the earth, which can drive a mill. There are many good fish in the water. Above the city, on a mountain, a new city developed, and a great beautiful church was built, the roof of which is covered with lead. In the choir of that church near the high altar there is a grave within a rock into which the Evangelist Saint John entered and never returned. The Evangelist Saint John was bishop in that city and performed many miracles. This church is now the Turks' department store,[202] and whoever wants to see the grave pays a Venetian ducat. In that city, they carry out the greatest barter with all kinds of goods, and everything is offered there, which is sold in the church.

At the time when the king of England and the king of France began the war,[203] the noble Christian lady to whom the city belonged lived there, together with her husband; she maintained an inn and offered wine which she sold to the Christians. The Turk who had conquered the city was called Zabalin,[204] about whom they continue to sing songs of praise in Turkey. Nearby, also on the coast, a new city emerged, which is called Altelot and belongs to the Turks, although it is populated mostly by Christian merchants; there are churches and monasteries. People from all over the world come to that city, and all kinds of goods are imported there from "Tatteren" [Mongolia].[205]

Not far away from that city, there flows a river, as big as the Rhine; it originates from Mongolia and flows through Turkey. [Merchants transport on it] silk and silk fabric, spices, wax, sugar, cotton, and other precious trading goods.

After Zabalin had died and his children had grown up, they invited in murderers and thieves, and evil people who had been expelled from many different countries. They departed with the Turks on pillaging raids through all countries.[206] They were joined by shepherds and peasants, house servants, and Christians from the villages, who were much worse [than all the others]; they burned down and stole everything of which they had knowledge. Before the outbreak of the plague, monks who had escaped from their monasteries accompanied them, and they were worse than anyone else. When the plague broke out,[207] they pillaged churches, monasteries, and altars, and they did not leave anything behind; they traveled also to Constantinople and plundered the Hagia Sophia[208] and threw away all sacred objects [relics] and took all the valuable treasures that they could find. But God then worked amazing wonders because wherever any of those gems appeared, the people's flow of blood stopped, and this lasted for a long time and was so widespread that the Muslims, Turks, and Christians did not allow them to get into their palaces. Then they [the robbers] rode to Sicily, to the most beautiful city called Messina, where the rumor about this had not yet spread. Then the plague spread into all countries, and the people died or became insane. But when the rumor spread, the people threw all their precious objects made out of gold and silver and their silk clothes out onto the street where they were stepped on and destroyed by carts and horses. No one was allowed or even wanted to take any of that. Finally, the wisest people among them advised them to send the relics and gems back to where they had been stolen from, and they killed those people who were still alive and insane and burned the ships. Subsequently, the great lords and the big cities grew together, the pope preached a crusade against them [the Turks] and they gained many lands from them.

On the Tatars [Mongols]

There are also other heathens who are called in Latin 'Tattari' and in German 'Tataren' [Tatars], who emerged following the birth of Our Lord in the year 1268.[209] Those were crazy heathens who had elected a blacksmith as their lord.[210] He had a brother called Halaam. They were always obedient to their lord, the blacksmith. When he ordered them to kill their own children, or to do anything else, they did it without any opposition. He departed on military campaigns with his people and conquered the entire world in the Orient up to the lands of the upper Danube. The Knights Templar and the kings of Armenia and other Christians rode out together against those heathens.

Those Tatars were people who lived in the desert. And they are such a mad people, both men and women; they have broad shoulders and broad faces and small eyes, and when they laugh, then you no longer see their eyes. The men have very little hair in their beards, and they have no holy scripture. But they believe in the immortal God and worship Him. And all the different kinds of Christians, about whom I reported above, live in their land, and those among the Tatars who want to convert to Christianity can do so publicly. There are now many churches and monasteries, friars and priests in that country, with the latter bringing with them the rich merchants so that everyone protects them. There is now a general custom in that country and in all cities and villages that all the Christians, Muslims, and Jews who live in a city gather with their bishop and with their priests. The bishop and the priest stand on a high chair and preach about the immortal God and the Christian faith, as they know how to do best.[211] Once a group of priests has preached, then another group steps up onto the chair and preaches against the other sermon, as they know how to do it best. The Tatars sit there, men and women, young and old, and listen to all the sermons, and the one sermon they like the best, that faith they can embrace.

The Jews are usually the first to preach; but they are immediately laughed at and proven wrong with their own scripture.

The members of the order of the preaching friars, the Augustinians and Carmelites, those who live there, purchase children with their money, who know all languages, as is customary there. And the merchants give them nomadic children whom they buy in all countries. Those children teach the friars their language so that the friars speak all the languages well. And the friars teach the children how to preach and how to answer all the questions they have written down in their books. That is what they teach the children, at first the *Pater noster* [the Lord's Prayer].[212] Some of them become very pious people who are very useful for the order. And since they are the property of the order, they cannot fight back or escape.[213]

The Tatars' clothing resembles that of the people of Armenia, but on their heads they wear a short and flat hat made out of felt, to which they attach a feather from a magpie, which are very valuable there. The merchants import them from distant countries, and those who cannot afford to purchase such feathers take a feather from another bird and must wear it always on their head out of obedience, because their first ruler once lost a battle and fled into bushes in which magpies rested. When the enemy followed him up to the bushes, they said to each other that no person could be there because if a person were in the bushes then the magpies would announce it, so they did not see him in the bushes. Therefore, the Tatar rulers ordered that there should not be any Tatar who would not wear out of obedience a feather from a magpie, or from another bird, in whatever country he would be, out of honor to the magpies. Those people continue to obey their lords very loyally; they are very brave and very good sharpshooters. Wherever they move to with all their might, they take with them wives and children, cows and calves, and sheep, from which they feed themselves whenever they are in the countryside or in front of a castle,[214] until they have conquered all. The women shoot as well as the men.[215]

When they want to give their daughters in marriage, the women run with a bow to the people on a market. The one who shoots best is the first to receive a husband. Wherever the Tatars move within their country to kings or lords, they are made easily discontented because what one grants them does not satisfy them.

In their country, the people do not buy and sell by means of gold or silver, but with small sheets of paper upon which is written the value of that paper. When that bill is used up [due to wear and tear], they give them another one as a replacement. They use all their gold and silver for jewelry and for large vessels. That country enjoys a very stable peace, and one can find there exquisite trading goods. Once a merchant has arrived there [and has purchased a large amount], he has enough for the rest of his life. But the people who want to travel there must make a huge detour because the

Sultan does not allow them to traverse the country directly, as the Muslims in his country travel there themselves.[216] All of the merchandise there is precious, of high quality, and affordable.

When the Tatars move around with full force, they do not return home unless they are dead or have gained the victory. They ride on small horses, and when they want to they cause the most harm by shooting arrows while galloping. They ride only with short stirrups.

The ruler of the Tatars is there called the emperor of Kathagien [Cathay],[217] and his correct title was the Great Khan, which means the Great Dog. He carries that name when he becomes emperor because he has fought viciously with all people in the Orient, and now there is an agreement between the emperor and Prester John that the first-born son of the one should marry the daughter of the other. When the Tatars embarked on their military campaign, they conquered much land from him and killed his son in a battle. Now they have struck this friendship between each other, which happened because of the Three Holy Magi, about whom there would be much to talk about.

But now, the emperor of Kathagien is the wealthiest and most powerful lord in the world, and the Sultan and all kings and rulers in Outremer [Near East] are not as mighty and as wealthy as he is alone, because he is the ruler of the entire country in which Asverus had been king.[218]

Now he is the ruler over all the countries that had belonged to Darius and Balthazar. He also controls the city and the kingdom of Nineveh[219] and Mesopotamia. There one of the Paradise rivers flows, the Tigris.[220]

The large city of Nineveh has long disappeared; it was situated on one side next to a mountain, and on the other on the shore of a great river, which flows from Paradise and is called Euphrates.[221] But not all the houses in the city were built next to each other; instead, they were all placed between the mountain and the river as if lined-up in a street. At times, the houses stood so far apart from each other that many vineyards and fields and other lands were located between them. But then again, other houses [serving different purposes] were erected close to each other so that no one could enter the city, either coming from the mountain or the water. In the past, the city had very beautiful walls and towers, and very attractive gates. There were also many beautiful churches and Christian monasteries. Finally, the Tatars conquered this city, and then Halaam, the emperor's brother, died.[222]

Moreover, the emperor of Kathagien possessed all the cities in India that used to belong to the Romans, and many beautiful areas that used to belong to Alexander the Great. In particular, he owned the mountains behind which Alexander locked in the Jews, and they guarded them particularly well to ensure that they would not escape.[223]

Further, the emperor controlled all countries that had belonged to Nebuchadnezzar.[224] The emperor owned three cities that the people praised as being more beautiful and more splendid than the entire kingdom of the Sultan, and those cities were called Baghdad, Thauris, and Cambeloch.[225]

The Caliph of Baghdad

In the city of Baghdad resides the caliph of the Muslims; that was their pope.[226] Each one who was elected [as a caliph] after Machomet is called by the Muslims a caliph, as the Christians call the one who is the successor to Saint Peter the pope. And at the time when the Tatars conquered all lands with their force, there was a king in Armenia called Hethum, who rode to the emperor of the Tatars with the intention of begging for mercy.[227] The Knights Templar accompanied him, and the emperor [of the Tatars] was very pleased that kings and lords from far away came riding to him to ask for mercy; and he welcomed them very honorably; and they stayed for two years with him. When they wanted to return, the emperor gave them a free choice: whatever pleased them, they should be granted. Then they begged him that he, along with his people, turn Christian, and that there should be eternal friendship between the Christians and the Tatars. They asked him to conquer Baghdad, Jerusalem, and the Holy Land, and to give that back to the Christians. All those things the emperor immediately carried out, and he gave them letters for what they had asked for, and he ordered his brother Halaam to ride with them and to conquer the Holy Land. When they got to Nineveh, Halaam died.

Then he ordered two important generals, each of whom commanded 30,000 Tatars, to go to Baghdad and besiege it for thirty days and nights without ever ceasing. [Indeed,] they conquered the city, and slew everyone who existed there; they only caught the caliph alive and they took him to the emperor and the Knights Templar, along with his entire treasure which was very large; in fact, so large that there has never been a human being who had ever witnessed so many treasures altogether. The emperor and the Knights Templar marveled at the treasure and asked the caliph why he did not pay enough people to protect the city with the help of the treasure. The caliph answered that evil counselors had convinced him not to do so because they told him that the women would certainly protect the city from the Tatars. Then they locked the caliph back in his room and threw gold, silver, and jewels to him and told him that such men who were to betray Machomet's teachings and would be pagan gods should not eat anything else but gold and jewels.

Thus he lived for thirteen days, and they took so many jewels and treasures from the city that the entire country is rich until today. There are not many gold and silver vessels in that country that do not originate from Baghdad, and afterwards there were no more caliphs among the heathens until the present day.

On Babylon

Half a French mile away from Baghdad there is the great Babylon, which is so close that one can see very clearly the ruins of the tower and the palaces and appreciate how large and how beautiful that city used to be. You can find many written documents about that.[228] But there is no one in that country who had visited it because there are many deep and dirty swamps as Babylon had been situated next to a great river from Paradise, called Euphrates. That river rises once a year to such a level that all the countryside around it is flooded. When the enemies conquered the city, they dug many ditches about a mile long around the city and led the water away through those, which allowed them to wade through. When the water gets into the ditches, it becomes bad and dirty. Many venomous snakes proliferate in the swamps so that no one can get through, and no one attempts to do so. Once the water rises again, then great ships arrive from India and bring very precious trading goods with them. The ships then steer so close to the city that the people on the stone walls and in the living-quarters can see all things. Baghdad is located at a higher elevation, which is now one of the most beautiful cities that exist in the world. It is very large, beautiful, and rich, and much could be said about it.

The emperor of Kathagien owns yet another city that is great and more powerful and beautiful, called Cambeloch. There are many thousand bridges leading into it. There would be much to report about it.

The Legend of the Barren Tree

The emperor owns yet another city that is called Susa in the Bible and is now called Thauris.[229] Ahasuerus lived in that city, and there the miracle happened of which you can read.[230] There is a barren tree in that city about which people recount many stories. The emperor hung his shield on that tree. People say that that tree had been standing there since the time of Abraham. But no one could say what kind of tree it was; it always remains in the same form and does not die or rot. From the olden days, much was won and lost in that country because of a custom, which they continue to observe strictly until today. When a ruler or a king was so powerful that he forcefully hung his shield [coat of arms] on the tree in defiance of the ruler of the country, then everyone accepted him without any opposition. But when a ruler had penetrated violently into the city and yet could not place his shield on the tree, they did not accept him as a ruler. They have fenced the tree in well and have it carefully protected. There is so much [more] to say about this tree and concerning so much fighting about this tree since the time of the Romans and other kings and rulers. Much has [already] been written about it.[231]

Government, Court, and Wealth of the Khan

The emperor runs his court much more sumptuously than Ahasuerus. He calls for a court assembly at the season when he was born, and when he rides somewhere. Then his people come along next to him on both sides for more than six miles. This fills all the cities and villages, which makes it impossible for anyone to move around and ride on horseback. Only the wisest and best ride next to the emperor; and wherever he crosses a city or a village, it looks as if it were burning with lots of smoke. The reason for that is that they burn spices, and the smoke of that rises there like a fog of [burned] herbs.

The emperor travels in a litter hanging between two elephants; his oldest son is seated next to him, and also his falconer and his favorite bird and hunting dogs. I could say much more about the beauty and splendor of the litter and all the equipment for the transport.

This noble emperor, who ruled in Tatary,[232] lived after the birth of Our Lord in the year 1340. He was a short, fat man and a courageous man, very humble in every regard and fearing God. He got to the city of Thauris where King Ahasuerus lived. There is a custom in that country: when the emperor approaches a city or a village, all men and women, young and old, come out to greet him with flutes and drums, and with string instruments. They dance to the best of their ability so that the emperor laughs, but no one is allowed to approach him without first giving him a gift, each according to his resources.

At the time when the emperor came to Thauris, the friars also approached him with their cross, and each one of them gave him an apple and they said that they did not have gold or silver, and that they could not and did not want to possess any. When the emperor had been told what kind of people they were, he left the litter and asked the friars to approach him. He took off his hat in front of them and accepted the apples with great humbleness and ate them; he also gave them to his son and to all the kings and lords and asked the friars to visit him at his court. There he had a special table arranged for them on the other side of his own. One had to step up to his table over three levels. On the upper level, there sat the emperor, the empress, and his eldest son; on the second level, there sat kings and queens, and on the third level there sat dukes, counts, and princes and their noble ladies. No human being would be able to grasp or report how beautifully and splendidly the palace was decked out with gold, silver, and jewels, and how impressive and spectacular everything was.

During the dinner, acrobats and masters of all kinds of talents performed, working with lions, animals, and birds, which they had trained to provide people with enjoyment. Once they had eaten, the friars said "Gratias," and when what they were saying had been translated to the emperor, he felt a very strong liking for them and let them sit with him and asked them to pray their "Benedicte" and "Gratias" in his language. He immediately ordered that it was written down, and wherever he went he said the "Benedicte" and "Gratias," and all people with him until today; he was a bold and good man.[233]

Wherever the emperor goes, they read to him during dinner all the texts dealing with the works and miracles that God had performed in the country in which Nebuchadnezzar, Ahasuerus, Xerxes, Balthazar, and Alexander had been rulers and where he now is the sole ruler. And he thanked God humbly that he had granted him the grace and the rule.[234]

The emperor of Kathagien owns more falconers and hunters than the Sultan, and in his country the dogs bark, which they do not do in other countries, and wherever he moves so many people go hunting with dogs and with birds of prey that no one can see or hear the others because of all the dogs.

The emperor of Kathagien rules over a particularly large country that used to be completely enclosed, in which special people live.

There is a unique island on which no one else lives but virgins, who have a queen. No man ever entered that country. But the virgins send messengers to their friends, and they themselves leave their country, and they ride with weapons and in great groups out of the country; they are very powerful and strong, and very skilled in shooting with bow and arrow. When the queen so desires, she rides out in a very impressive fashion. And when one of them stays with a king or a lord, no one can approach them in any way. When one of them gains a confidant [friend], then all the others love him as well, but when they become pregnant they lose a great part of their strength. They are very dark-skinned virgins with long brown hair; and they wear on their heads simple bands made out of gold; they are very sociable and friendly, and they have large limbs; wherever they stay, people give them much. But they do not demand that because they have enough of their own. So, they ride from one king to another. And their clothing and bows and arrows are very valuable, and some of them ride out of the country and back again, when the king so desires. When one of them delivers a daughter, they keep her with them in the country, but if it is a boy, they leave him behind in that country [where he was conceived], well-guarded until he has grown to maturity.[235]

In that country, there live women who ride with the same armed virgins; and the men stay home, spin the thread, and take care of the children.[236]

In that country, the virgins are the wooers, and the women pursue the young squires and men, as the men here in our country woo the women.

The emperor owns yet another country; very small people live there who fight with cranes. All people in the East and in the Orient lament the great problems they face with the cranes when those fly over their lands.[237]

There is yet another country subject to the emperor; the people who live there worship an idol whom they depict in their country, or wherever they live, in larger size than we paint the image of Saint Christopher.[238] They treat the idol with the greatest respect, and they would kill themselves on his behalf. When a virgin is prepared to do that, she hangs a sharp knife from her neck, and all virgins walk in front of her as if she were a bride, for three days, and this throughout the entire city, and this with the greatest ceremonial efforts. Then they walk to the idol in the temple, and she cuts her own throat. Her entire family is then proud of her deed. He who wants to worship the idol with his goods, brings and sacrifices to him the most beautiful and best treasure that he owns. The people in that country say that there might be more treasures made out of gold and gems in the temple than in any other country.

Additional paragraph in Ms. A (Ms. W261a): *The emperor also possesses another country. The people who live there eat only human flesh. The people [merchants] move around the country and buy all people, servants and maids who are worth nothing; they fatten them and stuff them like pigs, and sell them on the meat markets. The emperor owns yet another country that is called Paradise, and the people there say that apart from Paradise there is no more beautiful country in the world. He who is obedient to his lord is allowed to enter, and he who has earned that right to enter, or to get into that country, is the pride of his entire family. For that reason, everyone is obedient to the emperor and loyal in every respect [end of the textual addition].*

The emperor owns yet another country. The people who live there or wherever they exist believe that when a human being dies his soul moves into a wild animal. When he has been a good person throughout his life, then his soul enters a noble animal; when he has been an evil person, then his soul moves into a wolf, or a fox, or a non-noble animal. There are so many wild animals that are so tame that they go to the people's houses. The people attract them so that they return, and they treat them so well because they believe that the souls of their predecessors and relatives live in the animals; and no one is allowed to catch them. For that reason, the wild and the domestic animals roam [freely] throughout the country.[239]

The emperor rules over yet another country. The people who live there have talons on their fingers, longer and sharper than those of an eagle. With those they kill wild animals, and they defend themselves against those great animals. They are so fast in running that they catch up with animals. Those people eat raw meat.

The emperor owns yet another country that is flooded. The people who live there swim under the water and catch fish which they eat raw, like otters do.

The emperor controls yet another country that has now become Christian. There, they have a custom that when a woman is pregnant, she lies in childbed for three weeks, and the husband then lies in childbed for another three weeks. As he has taken care of her, so she treats him then.

All those extraordinary and strange people who get there and are sent there live all the time at the lords' and kings' courts.[240] **They believe that we are just as strange as they appear to us.**[241]

No one can list and fully comprehend the other countries, treasures, and wonders that the emperor of Kathagien possesses.

The Persians

Moreover, in Outremer, there is yet another group of heathens who are called Persians. They do not have any law, but they request permission to walk with the Christians into their churches. Wherever they live, either among Muslims or Christians, they accept the faith of those who live closest to them. That country is called Persia. All monks, merchants, and all people who want to travel to India must cross it first. They have to travel in large groups because the Muslims who used to live there did not like to allow monks or merchants to traverse their country. The monks had to put on different clothing. When the merchants and the Christians had assembled thus,[242] the Muslims got together to face them collectively, but they could not force the Christians to return. Hence, they demand a very high tribute [toll] for the permission to pass through. Nevertheless, they receive little. When they demand 1000 gold ducats, they receive less than 20.[243] They cannot do anything evil against the Christians because of the emperor of Kathagien.

Translation

PART II – GENERAL INFORMATION ABOUT THE ORIENT

Climate and Vegetation

After our report on and discussion of the countries in Outremer, the cities and peoples who live there, the kings, princes, and lords who reside there, and their countries, next follows a report about the conditions of the lands there.

First, you need to know that the land in Outremer is oddly structured. It is mostly located in the mountains, and at those elevations no one can distinguish well between summer and winter. At those heights in the mountains there is always winter, and throughout the year, both in winter and in summer, there is much snow. The people press the snow hard together [ice] and export it to the cities and sell it to the lords so that they can cool their drinks, but it melts quickly. While it is extremely cold in the mountains, at their feet the heat is unbearable.

It rarely rains in that country [region], but in Egypt it rains neither in winter nor in summer. And when it rains during the summer once or twice, then people feel very happy, and when it rains during winter once or twice,[244] then in the following years people will not suffer from a drought. But when it does not rain in winter, then a drought can easily happen, and then no grain can ripen during the year.

From Michaelmas[245] onwards, grass and plants begin to grow, and are then followed by wheat and rye. Hence, people harvest both in the middle of the winter, but during the summer no plant can grow because of the extraordinarily intense heat, unless they irrigate them, or they grow at a place where the sun does not shine.

In the winter, there are many earthquakes, but not in all cities or at all times; they happen mostly at night. Many cities and castles there have fallen apart and are lost, and many mountains have split. Therefore, people lament greatly,[246] and the women throw off all their jewels. However, once the quake is over, then they fetch them again. During the day, all people act like we do on Good Friday, repenting greatly and fasting.[247]

Throughout the entire winter, there is thunder without rain.

When it rains once during winter, then grain and plants grow during a day or during a night higher than a span.[248]

From the feast day of the Three Holy Magi [Jan. 6] until Shrovetide,[249] roses and beans grow, amongst others; you rarely find peas.

In March, April, and May, the grain ripens, but at some heights earlier and at others later, depending on whether the country is low or high. At some elevations, they grow grapes throughout the entire winter, skillfully tying them to sticks. At some other elevations, the old fruit stays on the trees until the new fruit begins to grow on the same one.[250] Throughout the entire winter, they grow strawberries and other fruit which are cooling for the people [in terms of the four humors].

The grain is seeded not more than two fingers apart in the soil so that it does not burn in the earth.

From April until Michaelmas, the heat is so intense that grass and plants that had grown during winter burn up, unless they are located where the sun does not reach them.

All people walk or ride on horseback from Vespers throughout the night until the early morning.[251]

From the early morning until Vespers, you never or rarely see any person in the fields and in the streets because of the excessive dust. When a wind rises from the west, which is cold, the people appreciate it, but when it blows from the east or the south, then it is so hot that no one can stay in the fields or in the streets.

In the cities, the people cover the streets with sheets or with appropriate mats, just as everyone can afford it, and they sweep the streets and wash them with water. There are poor people who carry around cold water, herbs, and cold fruit in the streets and sell those so that the people cool themselves down. Another group of poor people carry incense and cinnamon on a hot plate so that the streets are filled with smoke.[252] Poor people get their food from that.

When people go out into the street, then they all carry cloths filled with the smell of precious herbs [scented]. They hold them in front of their noses. All people wear robes out of light linen that they spread out in front of their beds during the night and that are scented with precious herbs.

Clothing, Appearance, and Living Conditions of Those Living in the East

All virgins and women wear eye make-up, which lasts until they cry; then the paint disappears because of the tears, and there are then old women who can paint it all over again.

All virgins and women have only one braid which they entwine with gold and pearls; and all the women's shoes are flat and elegant.

All the men's and women's clothing is made according to the customs of their country. But all linen robes are thoroughly bleached; flax grows there twice a year and is very affordable; and the women's clothing is tight and white according to their local customs and sometimes according to the French fashion [imported from Europe]. The women's outerwear is very long so that it extends by two or three *Ellen*.[253] Whatever is placed on top of the clothing is entwined very elegantly with gold or with pearls. When noble ladies go riding on horseback, then the servants follow them carrying their outer garment. And when they go on foot, then they carry the outer garment under their arms, and the maid carries the other part behind them. All men and women, whether noble or not noble, are constantly on the move there, but no one is ashamed of it because it is their common custom.[254]

All princes and lords who used to live in Acre and its environs, knights and merchants, and their wives, wear clothing like that in France, and the women dress even more splendidly when they attend court. But when they walk in the street somewhere else, or ride on horseback, then the women wear black coats, which they have worn since the time when Acre was conquered.[255] They wish to wear them until Our Lord God returns the country and the city to them.

The wedding celebrations are very elaborate and lengthy. Although it is daytime, they carry candles before the bride, and you see many beautiful jewels, and then, although men and women come together, they rarely eat and drink together. But at night, they sleep together, and when they have daughters, they raise them very carefully, each according to his/her abilities, until they marry them off.

He who has a guest at dinner time takes good care of him. They offer many different types of bread, and this at an affordable price.

All foods are sold on the market there, including meat from both wild and domestic animals, whatever a person desires, and this for a good price. Apart from kings and lords, no one is so wealthy that they bake in their own house. All knights and lords give monthly stipends to their servants for food. But bread and meat are handed out from the court [kitchen] when they are outside of the castle. Everything concerning their clothing and food is very clean since otherwise the people could not stand the heat and stay healthy.

The Christians there drink wine, and the Muslims drink water, which is very good and a healthy practice.[256]

In the entire country of Outremer, no one owns castles or fortresses except for the Sultan, the kings, and the princes. The lords and knights live in the villages in the countryside, enjoying their lives at their own estates and personal properties. These aristocrats go hunting with dogs and birds of prey; they know of no discomfort and help their lords in time of need. The people erect, without great effort, very attractive great stone columns because they have molds made out of wood, depending on how big the column or stone monument is supposed to be. Then they bake small stones which they pick up from the water [pebbles], break them into small pieces, and place those pieces in the molds and pour a handful of water on them which is useful for it. Thus, the mold is shaped immediately, becomes hard, and when they open the mold, then the stone column remains, and the stones rest. In this way, they very easily build in India wonderful and great castles, towers, and palaces.[257]

The soil in that country is very loose because of the great heat, and when it rains twice a year, the drops that fall are so big that one drop alone penetrates all clothing. Then it rains so hard that a great flood comes rushing down from the mountain, and this so quickly that it rips away, within a few hours, large cities and villages, and then all the lands and all the cities remain devastated for a long time.

All princes, lords, knights, and merchants throughout the lands up to India speak French, but the peasants in the villages speak their country's own idiom.[258]

All the property which the lords own is feudal property [loaned] for which they must become knights. Once the youngsters have grown up and are to be knighted, then all lords, princes, and their relatives assemble, and all those whom the applicant can ask to come, one month before the event, join in. Then he rides, splendidly dressed, behind the city and lies down on a beautifully decked bed. Then the noble lords arrive and lift him up, dress him in precious robes and vestments, and equip him with his sword and his spurs and ride splendidly around the city,[259] to find out if someone might come and accuse him of some evil deed, which would prevent him from becoming a knight. The next day, they make him into a knight, just as it is done in our country. Then they hold a great court, and they [obviously the new young knights; here in plural] then have to behave properly in the future so that nothing evil will be said about them and no bad rumors spread.

The income of a knight consists of 1000 bezants,[260] each bezant worth two ducats. With that, they maintain two horses and appear twice a day before the palace, but the servants' salaries go up and down.[261] When they go hunting with their lords or leave the castle with the weapons, they receive food and fodder from the court.[262]

It is the custom in all Christian countries not to deny any foreign knight the specific salary which he expects. And the one who demonstrates his bravery will fare well with all lords in whose company he spends his time. Those lords then immediately recognize what the man is capable of doing.

In the Sultan's country, the knights neither know of quintain[263] nor of tournaments and are familiar only with hunting with dogs and hunting with birds of prey and pursue otherwise their physical health. But where the Christians, princes, lords, and knights live who had previously lived in Acre, there they do the quintain, the tournament, and pursue a very splendid and often courtly lifestyle.[264]

Translation

Further, neither the Sultan nor a Christian king can transfer any power to a knight, unless this happens with the approval of the other knights, or if the people rise up, or assemble for a special occasion.[265]

No knight is allowed to kill a man unless he has been referred to the council [legal court] and his guilt has become obvious.

Further, one must report once a week to the Sultan or to the other Christian kings everything about the people who are imprisoned there, and about their crimes.

All kings, Christians and Muslims, have people who earn an income through writing down all misdeeds and all events and miracles that happen in the world and in the various countries at their time.

There are other people who write down all misdeeds which the knights have committed, and when the time has come, then they read them all out aloud in front of the people, and neither money nor pleading can prevent that [shamefulness], and so they have to give up their lives.[266]

The legal courts issue very strict judgments on the rich and poor, each according to his guilt. This applies particularly to the case of killing, for which there is no other payment but one's own life, unless it had happened as the result of an accident or misfortune. If a man is killed through an accident, or is thrown to his death, then the closest relatives of the dead say before the court to the one who has actually killed their relative that he would not be the one they blame for the deed. Instead, the true culprit had escaped into a foreign country, and the one here at court would compensate the relatives for the killing.

When someone is injured, then the judge describes the wound and what kind it is. If the injured man dies, then all the medical doctors who are present have to testify whether he died of the wound or whether he could have been healed.

There are many artists who play string instruments, drums, and flutes, as has been the case for a long time, as one can read in the book,[267] but here in this country it is all much better and more skillful. All the services are carried out according to many different customs because so many people of different cultures live there. This makes it impossible to comprehend each custom.[268]

No one can sell there any kind of herbs, silk, silken cloth, and jewels, pearls, theriac,[269] and other things unless they are first examined by people who have been sworn in on this job and who are employed to determine whether anything is falsified, because a heavy penalty would be imposed in such a case. None of the money and none of the coins fall short in weight, which they used to in the past.

Among Christians and Muslims, there are freedoms [privileges, or rules]. When someone who has suffered an accident [has committed an evil deed by accident] is required to make compensation, the judge must swear that he will not condemn him to death. But he will remove his social rank; he is then imprisoned, and he receives only water and bread until his death.

When someone has been condemned to death, then his friends lament for him in the same way as if he had died in his bed.

When they want to kill [execute] a man of noble origin, [they lead him to the execution site] the judge and the complainants walking behind him, with bare legs, and they do not wear anything but a shirt, and they walk without wearing anything on the head.

Then, it is a common custom among Christians, Jews, and Muslims that when a person has died, then all the friends cry and lament for him. There are then women who lament his life correspondingly, and they scratch themselves and tear out their hair. Once the women have sung a verse, then the friends wail and tear out their hair. You find many old women who have pulled out their hair who are now bald.

Merchandise that is exported across the sea [to Europe]: spices, sugar, silk, cotton, silk fabric, gems, pearls, and all kinds of other valuable goods.

Merchandise that is exported to Outremer: fabric, fur clothing, iron, lead, large horses from Spain, great bells from Venice and Germany.

They also import resin glue with which they make bows, and also falcons, and similar goods.

Exotic Animals

Now that I have talked and written about the people who live in Outremer,[270] that is, about their customs and actions [deeds], the next topic will be the animals that exist there. You must know that all animals, both the wild and the domestic ones in that country, are more beautiful and much larger than the animals in our country. There are the following animals, which are rare back home and very common here [in the Near East]: lions, dragons, elephants, tigers, salamanders, leopards, dromedaries, camels, antelopes, wild donkeys, buffaloes, wild rams, wildcats [mountain lions, or pumas], giraffes, belechs,[271] and crocodiles.[272] But there are not many bears

Translation

in that country, or many wolves, unless they are brought there or shipped in.

The lion is a noble animal which people in that country have often seen in its natural environment[273] and which is discussed extensively in books.[274]

The leopard is a clean animal; it eats only fresh meat, like a falcon; and it is tame and rides after its master placed on a horse, beautifully covered, and dressed like a falcon; it is delightfully decorated all over its body. The servants must keep it clean; it is very sociable, and when its lord is asleep, it does not allow any person to approach him.[275]

A unicorn exists only in India, and the local people say that it is very large and that its horn is so heavy that a man could barely lift it from the ground. It is very sharp.[276] It is a beautiful animal, blue in color, and its head is formed like that of a goat; and its feet are like those of a pig. It cannot tolerate any dirt.

A panther is a small animal (with beautiful fur),[277] delicately decked in all colors of the rainbow, that is, in all colors that exist here on earth, and so subtly that no one can replicate that completely [in a painting]; it also smells good. After panthers die, kings and princes use their furs to cover the floor next to their beds because their smell protects against all evil. They do not exist in any other country but India, and they do not eat anything else but special plants. All animals follow their breath. When a panther becomes angry, it harms people. It is an animal with great bodily heat and the strength of the special plants [herbs] whose aroma streams out of its mouth. Wherever the panther moves, all evil animals and snakes leave.

The antelope is an extraordinarily nervous animal,[278] formed like a goat; it has feet like a dog and horns like a ram which are sharper than a saw, which allow it to cut down a tree. It must live near running water, and when it espies its shadow, it jumps back and forth and is so delighted about it. People there create fences out of small sticks to which are attached strong ropes, and when the antelope then jumps and plays in that way, it gets caught in the sticks and ropes. There would be no other way of catching it.

The tiger is a noble animal. It causes much harm and is evil and so fast that no person can catch it or chase it away. But when people manage to take away its small ones, then it does not stay in the country. When it runs into the people who want to rob it of its young ones to make money, it is baffled by a large mirror which they bring with them. Once they have taken the young ones, they place a mirror at that site and wipe it with the bodies of the cubs, and when the parent animals then arrive, they smell and look into the mirror. They then lose all interest and believe that they have lost one of their cubs and continue chasing after it on the trail. When the mother then returns[279] to where the people have placed the mirror, she looks into it, and believes she has found her two cubs. She then cries so much because of the smell that it takes a long time, and she runs around the mirror. In the same way, she runs around the mirror as many times as she had cubs, and when the animal [tigress] believes she has gotten the cubs together, they [again in plural] become so confused that the people who have removed the cubs escape from there. When the tigresses notice that they have been cheated out of the cubs, they depart from the country out of sorrow[280] and never return. There are no other strategies to get rid of the tigers.

The salamander is a small animal and is rarely seen alive. It lives in the desert in the hot sand and raises its small ones in the soil. It has as many feet as a caterpillar. Its skin is as white as that of a hermelin [ermine]. It does not burn in the fire, and every year it renews itself [gets a new skin], and it is small and soft like a silk cloth. People use that skin to give to the princes and lords after dinner like a herb, and when they want to go to sleep.

A wild goat lives in the desert and is built like a donkey. It is a very clean animal. It throws its foals out of the lair using its teeth, but not the oldest male. But when that one dies or is caught, then it does not throw away the male that had been born second.[281] The lords very much enjoy hunting this animal because no other animal exists in such great numbers when it is hunting time. He who eats this meat and is not used to it does not keep it in his stomach.

A wild ram is just like a tame one, but it is much bigger and built like a deer. It develops a layer of fat deeper than a finger all over its body. It has very attractive large horns, and these animals walk together in the forest and in the fields like tame sheep in great groups. They run so hard toward a tree that it breaks, and through their running they create a strong wind so that you can perceive it from far away, but when the dogs or the leopards chase after them, they do not defend themselves.[282]

The belech is built like a fawn and has an extraordinarily long tongue, and on the tongue there are very sharp outgrowths [teeth?] with which it licks[!] the bark of the trees. When people hunt that animal it stands still in front of the dogs and defends itself with its tongue, and only then is it shot dead. When it is dead, its tongue is as smooth as the tongue of another animal.

Translation

People do not eat anything else from that animal but the tongue and become very strong from it.

A giraffe is like a deer, but its front part is taller than the back part. It has feet like a horse, and a neck longer than twelve feet. It has a hump and horns like a roebuck. After it has been caught, they put a ring through the nostrils which makes them as tame as they like. It is tall like a deer, very noble, and it is kept at the courts of kings and princes. They put burning candles on its horns, and in this way they illuminate the entire hall.

The buffalo is built like the large oxen as they exist in our country. It has very broad horns, not much fur, and its skin is much thicker than a finger (they have a ring in their nose).[283] When they are tame, then they are very kind, and when you want to milk them, then you call each one of them by their names, after which they come. People make cheese from their milk, which is fibrous like beef, and when they are wild and people hunt them, they get into such a rage that they chase the hunters and the dogs all the way into the cities, and they follow those who wear a red dress even into their houses.

The elephant is a large, extraordinarily gruff animal.[284] Further north in India, the elephant is much larger and has hair like a horse. It can be as easily killed and butchered as a horse. It devours more than twelve baskets of barley per day, and it probably needs four times as much straw. When people spend time with the elephants in the field, they cut down large trees and branches as food for them. Its teeth are so long and so great that it mostly cannot lower itself down to the ground.[285] But the people hang a large white bag just a little in front of its trunk, which it picks up from the ground, bends, and thus pushes into its mouth what it wants to eat. When it drinks, it must stand deeply in water, and it drinks more than two *amen* of water all at once.[286] It becomes so tame that when its master plays a whistle for it, it dances. And when the master says that it should welcome the people, then it bows its head before the people. And when its master orders that it die, it falls down, and when he tells it to return from death, then it gets up again.

It has a neck and a tail like a pig, and its ears are like a tub, and it is so strong that people place towers on its neck,[287] made out of thin sticks. Those are covered inside and outside with cloth, at the bottom wide, at the top narrow; there are three layers that have room for the king's bed and his entire equipment, plus about twenty men with stones and other projectiles, which they shoot and throw. Its master sits between the elephant's ears, and he holds a large hammer [stick] in his hand with which he prods the animal onward. On its neck there is room for six men. It has feet like a dog and nails like a human being; it does not have a middle joint in the legs like other animals, and when they want to march into war with it, then they have to armor it. When they give it blood or red wine to drink, it falls into a great rage and does not shy away from breaking through barriers. The enemies have created vessels made from clay which they fill with glowing coals, and those they roll in front of the animals, which burn them so that they fall down.

Its little ones are seven times larger than a great Frisian ox, and none of the bones in its body are worth as much as its teeth [tusks]. The elephant that originates from India is so big that no human being can push it [or make it move]. The people say that it cannot bend down; but that is not true because it certainly bends down and gets up; the noise which they then make sounds as if a house is collapsing.[288]

When it has calves, it must take them to islands in the sea to avoid dragons that can catch them. No animals hate each other more than the dragon and the elephant.

A dragon is in its physical appearance a very clean animal; it is character- ized by many stripes as in a rainbow; its head looks like that of a greyhound, and its wings like those of a bat. Its flight does not last for long, and when the time comes when they are in heat, they bite each other so badly that they die. For that reason, one rarely or never sees them. But in the desert you notice them well, where they have passed through with their tails in the sand. They look extraordinarily poisonous. When they find one of them dead, they cut off the head and bury the body.[289]

The camel is a very extraordinary animal, very large and gruff, as tall as a man can stand up; it has a long neck and short ears, its stomach is very large, its feet are very small, and it has a hump on its back. It has small feet and two claws like an ox, and it is so extraordinarily well-tempered that a child can easily control a hundred camels. Each one is connected to the other by its tail, and when the first gets up, then all the others get up. When the first starts moving, then they all go, and what the front animal does, they all do, and when thousands of them are together, they would never bite or hit each other; they only grunt when they greet each other. But at the time when they neigh, or when people want to tame wild camels, then they are very dangerous. They drink only once every third day, and they eat less than a donkey; they carry everything that people can load upon them. When a camel's master loads it, it sits down, and when it is then loaded and its master speaks, it gets up. It has large calluses below the chest and below the knees. It is so stupid that it won't find the stable again in which it has lived. And the calves, which are wild, walk along with the tame animals until they are tame as well. They do not run but rather ambulate calmly and make wide strides. In August, they lose all of their fleece so that they are completely naked all over the body and cannot tolerate any cold.

A dromedary is built like a camel in every regard, but it is much larger, higher, longer and better tempered. They are faster and walk very quickly and stride widely. He who rides one reaches his goal for sure in the duration of a day.

A wildcat is like a leopard, and when it is young no one can know whether it is a wildcat or a leopard. It is as large as a hunting dog, and when in the forests it jumps from one tree to another, like a squirrel. When it is more than a year old and touches anyone with its claws, making a drop of blood come oozing out, whether this is a human being or any other creature, that victim has to die. No medicine can prevent that. The wildcats mostly exist in Armenia, and when you want to hunt there, you move with an elephant and the armored tower into the forest, and where the elephant is to stand still the people fill all the trees with movable nets, and then the lords and people hunt any wild animals that they can find. When there are wildcats, the people notice that through the [reaction of the] dogs. Then both people and dogs run away to the elephants. The wildcats, however, follow them up to where the elephants are. Then they jump into the ropes and into the nets, whereupon the people stab and shoot the wildcats. There is no other way to catch them. Neither people nor dogs fear any other animal more than the wildcats.

A crocodile is an extraordinarily dangerous animal; it is very strong and horrifying. It is bigger than an ox in size. Its fur is like that of a wolf; it lives in Egypt in the great river called Nile, which flows from Paradise. The crocodile is a terrifyingly fast and harmful animal. Whatever it grabs outside of the water, such as people, horses, or other animals, it drags into the water. The prey that was in the water[290] it pulls out onto the land and eats it there. On the land it is like a wolf, and in the water it is like an otter. There is neither any advice nor any skill for how to chase it away. People certainly take away its hatchlings [but to no avail]. It is so strong that it [can] push down large ships in the water. At the time when Acre was still held [by the Christians], the Knights Templar had a crocodile from whose mouth they had pulled the teeth and which they had tamed. It [could] pull a stone to a building site which ten men could not lift from the ground. However strong this animal is, a small snake always follows it which is as large as a caterpillar. It follows it constantly, and it greatly fears that snake. It follows the crocodile into the water where it swallows it along with other fish. The snake then bites its heart apart so that the crocodile dies. There is much written about the crocodile in the *Vitae Patrum*.[291]

The horses in Outremer are not greater than those that you buy at the price of twelve or sixteen guilders; they are very strong, useful,[292] and fast. The large horses come from Spain and Venice. Then there are yet other types of horses which are not much larger than those you can buy for sixteen ducats. Those come from India and are very expensive. They are particularly fast, and he who can let them run might be able to catch deer and does, but only the Sultan and the kings own those kinds of horses because you pay 10,000 florins for them.[293] They are very fast. He who does not know how to ride on them well loses his senses [becomes terrified or discombobulated] when seated on them.

All tame animals there are just like those here at home, but they are much larger over there. The sheep and goats and all those kinds of animals have young ones twice a year, and sometimes more than just one. The fat that the sheep and rams have on their body, those [in Outremer] have in their tail, and sometimes so much that there is as much fat deposited there as in the entire body. [If I had more room], there would be much more to say about the other animals, domestic or wild, which are common there and rare here.

Hunting Animals

A report about hunting practices follows this account of the animals. You need to know that in the country of Outremer the hunting dogs are of the same kind as here [back home]. There is one caretaker for every two dogs, who does nothing else but watch them. He gives them a bath, combs them, keeps them clean,[294] and supplies them properly with neck leashes and all other equipment. And the dogs are tied to ropes both day and night and rest on very clean carpets. But in the morning and in the evening the caretakers lead them to the field and let them run; they do not consume anything else but rye bread. But each lord who likes a particular dog calls it to the dining table and throws at it a coarse slice of bread.[295]

The dogs do not run around freely, but when the lords want to go hunting, then they take from one hundred to two hundred peasants from the villages and place the dogs at a distance from the leopards. Then the peasants move into the bushes, beat [drums] and shout, and then the wild animals run toward the dogs which are very fast, and the dogs then cut the throats of what they catch, whether it is a small or a large animal. The wild animals that escape from the dogs get in front of the leopards, which rest in the ropes and observe all that. When the wild animals approach the

Translation

leopards, then the latter jump as fast as an arrow and catch the animals with their claws. When the wild animals run toward the leopards, no dog follows them. What the leopards catch, they hold in their jaws. Then both lie quietly on the ground. Then the master arrives and kills the wild animal, gives the head to the leopard, and takes the body with him.

The leopard makes only three jumps at a time, and what it does not catch in that triple move it then ignores, whether it stands or lies there. But it walks back and forth and is very enraged and angry when its master then follows it. The latter must not approach it until the leopard has turned around and come to its master.

There are no other dogs but greyhounds. Those greyhounds that are imported from overseas do not run during the summer, but they do not run much in the winter either.[296]

Birds

In the country of Outremer there are all the wild and tame birds [known], but in the case of all birds and animals, the higher the elevation of where they exist the larger and more beautiful they are, in opposition to the people who are so much smaller the higher up they live.

The birds that are common there and rare here are the following: eagle, ostrich, pelican, flamingo, common quail, francolin, parrot, phoenix, caradrius, and many other birds.

The eagle is a beautiful, noble, and large bird, as everyone knows. In those countries, they are so trained that people can go hunting doves with them, and similar birds, but there are two masters assigned to one eagle, and those are in turn supported by two servants; those carry crutches which they place underneath the eagle.

The ostrich is a very large bird, and further north they are larger and more noble, and they are as tame as cranes, and their body is as large as a barrel. They have a long neck like a crane, and a beak like a goose, and legs that are as thick as a human arm. They have hardly any feathers. Its few feathers are thin, and it does not fly; instead, it runs very quickly, and when it is in the wild, people chase it with dogs in particular. Underneath its wing it has a sharp hook, longer and sharper than a rooster's talon. When the ostrich is being hunted, it hits itself with the hook, which allows the hunters to track it via the blood. When it is wild in the desert, it lays its eggs in the hot sand and places a rock on top of them so that no one can see or find the eggs. When it has placed all the eggs there, the parent birds stand above the eggs and gaze toward the sun so that the reflection of the sun falls onto the eggs. From those then develop the hatchlings, and this so quickly that the eggshells sit tightly on their heads. They have very angry eyes. When the young ones leave with the old ones, the ostrich takes the stone again and places it in such a way that you can see where its nest and its eggs had been. Its eggs can hardly ever, or never, be found, because they cannot be detected in the sand. At the kings' and the lords' courts, they do not let those go [guard them closely]. People do not believe at all that anyone in the world might eat eggs from ostriches. Those are much bigger than a human head.[297]

The ostriches at the courts of the lords eat rye and whatever they give them, like a crane. They enjoy being where the people [farriers] put new shoes on horses. These craftsmen give them the old nails from the shoes.[298]

The pelican is a bird as tall as a crane and built like it. It loves its young ones so much that it tears them apart out of its great love, scratching them with its claws so that they die. Then it cuts open the right side between the ribs with its beak and lets its own blood drip on the young ones, which revives them.[299]

A flamingo is a bird that wants to be in water constantly; it is very clean and not quite as large as a swan. It has white and red plumage.

A common quail looks like a chicken and is about the same size; the female is grey and has a red head. They are more noble than the francolin and as common as any other bird. Their price is affordable, so that you can buy three for a Venetian ducat. People who live in the countryside own tame common quails. They provide wine for them to drink and tie them to a stick in the field. That then lures the other wild common quails, and when those have come to the tame ones they bite each other so that at the end they lie on each other, dead, in large piles. When a tame quail is overwhelmed, it no longer defends itself, and the tame ones that know how to fight well are especially expensive and desired; they constitute very valuable meat. God let the quails come to the children of Israel when they desired meat while they were in the desert.

A francolin is a bird as small as a pigeon and has feathers like a pheasant. It lives in grain fields like a quail and utters a strange sound.[300] This bird is regarded as the most noble one in that country. People catch it with nets like those with which we catch quails.

A parrot is a small bird with green feathers which does not fly long distances. It learns all languages within a year,[301] until a red stripe grows at its neck. Once that has grown fully, it cannot learn a language, and it is a bird that is

Translation

very weak on its feet. This means that it cannot climb without the help of the beak. People raise the parrot as a tame bird and sell it in large numbers. When the parrots are young, they are sold for two Venetian ducats; when they are wild, then people raise the young birds at a body of water, which they do not like at all. They cannot fly for a long distance.

The phoenix is a bird that is not commonly seen in that country.[302] But kings and princes appear to have phoenix feathers. Those they pass on to their children. These feathers are very beautiful and of such an extraordinary color that one cannot describe it.[303] But people there say that the phoenix does not exist anywhere in the world but in Arabia.[304]

The caradrius[305] is a rare bird, and it is very expensive and much sought after. It is built like and is the size of a duck. Those birds fly around in India, and there are not many of this species. When a person suffers from a bad illness, then the doctors have the bird push its beak into the mouth of the sick one, which sucks all the sickness out of their body. As long as the bird does that, the sick one stays quiet, but when the bird no longer wants to do so, or cannot do it anymore, hence then turns away from the sick person; then there is no longer any hope for the person, who must [certainly] die.[306]

Chickens and pigeons and other domestic birds are raised there, just as here, but they are much bigger. The chickens in India have a body that is as large as a crane, but they do not grow tall and have a red head and feathers like a sparrow hawk when it molts. I could say much more about other animals that are common in Outremer and are rare here in [Germany].

In our land, birds exist that are rare in Outremer. Those are the storks, which cannot be found abroad, unless they are imported there.[307]

Further, there are not many geese, which exist in that country only at the courts of kings and princes.

Swallows arrive there in March, as they do here.[308]

There is a small bird that flies above water and feeds on fish; it is called *Yseren Bart*.[309] All princes and lords there desire to own one of these small birds, and they talk a great deal about it when they meet in a group.

In the country of Outremer, there are no falcons; only near Babylon was there a nest of a sparrow falcon. The reason is that there are so many large eagles that the falcons cannot survive in that country. But all gyrfalcons and other falcons that exist there and in the entire Orient originate from Norway and Prussia, and from Flanders, imported by people who trade with them. The Sultan demonstrates great kindness to them whenever they arrive there. When one of those birds dies during the transport, he would

Der Niederrheinische Orientbericht, c.1350

still give them enough money for the dead bird [maybe out of respect or financial commitment?]. No one can continue going hunting with falcons, neither in the countryside nor at the rivers, because the eagles do not allow the falcons to fly in the air, unless there are so many of them together, as I have described above regarding the Sultan's hunting.[310]

Otherwise, they go hunting with birds of prey, holding them on their fist,[311] such as with a sparrowhawk. When another falconer arrives, their skill comes to an end.[312] It is a common custom at all the lords' courts, that when a noble dog comes to the court of a lord, the gatekeeper kills it, and they feed the falcons with the meat. All falconers are servants of the lords. There are so many partridges[313] and breeding chickens which no one is allowed to chase away. All falconers carry long whips with them while riding on horseback, with which they hit those birds when they fly ahead of the falcons.[314]

Plants and Fruit

In the country of Outremer, all trees bear fruit as they do here, but not all fruit can grow there, unless the farmers treat it with great skill because much of the fruit rots while still on the tree. The fruit and trees that are common there and rare here are: the wooden aloe, cedar, cypress, *sichim*,[315] Paradise apples, pistachio, pharaoh's figs,[316] asparagus, pepper, sugar cane, cotton, incense, thyme, palm trees, carob trees, pumpkin, rice, and nutmeg.

The cedar tree is a noble tree and much taller than a fir tree but built the same way. It smells wonderfully well and has cones like a fir tree, but those are much larger, and where a cedar grows there cannot exist any evil poison or any snake. It grows up to 100 feet tall before it develops even one branch. Even when the wood rests for a thousand years in water or in the open air, it does not decay or rot. It is not easy to cut it down or to saw it unless special masters who know their business do it.

The cypress is also a very tall and noble tree; it looks in every way like a cedar, but the difference is in the smell.

The palm tree is an extraordinarily tall tree, and it grows in an odd fashion because at first all the branches grow out of the soil as strongly as they are supposed to, then the palm grows two feet per year or more, and the branches then grow like a crown around the tree. When it is fifty years old, the fruits grow next to the branches; they are called *Datteln* [dates].[317] They grow out of the trees like grapes during Shrovetide, and when they get bigger they hang off the trees and are so large and heavy that they drop off the trees. A bunch of them is so large that a man can [barely] lift it from

Translation

the ground. The tree is full of these bunches, all around the top, up and down, and the palm leaves that the pilgrims bring with them are the young shootings of the trees; the branches, however, are very large.

The wood of the sikkim tree looks like that of the oak tree, black as pitch.[318] It attracts the cold and takes many advantages and virtues from the sun at its top. It removes all swellings, and people write that it cannot be burned in a fire because of the cold in it.[319]

The Brunzilia wood[320] grows mostly on the islands, where there is a lot of reed, especially in the Red Sea. There is much other red wood without an inner marrow.

No one can show us where the aloe tree grows because [only] large pieces of it come flowing down the river which originates in Paradise [Nile]. It grows tall and is like a dry wood that has fallen from a hill into a body of water.[321]

Paradise apples grow on a tree that has no branches, but it has leaves that are at least six to eight ells long.[322] And the tree and the leaves are deeply green during summer, but when the leaves are very long and wide, then the wind immediately blows them off. The tree is as big as two men, and the apples grow in thick groups next to the leaves. They are green, and there are about a hundred together on a branch. They taste like fresh butter, and the middle of the apple looks like a crucifix. Those apples cannot be kept for a long time.[323]

The Adam's apple is a very nice fruit;[324] it is colored golden-yellow and larger than a child's head. In the apple, there is a mark [wound] as if a person had bitten into it with his teeth. On the outside, it looks very beautiful, but on the inside it is very bitter. The people there believe that Adam and Eve transgressed God's ban with this fruit. These apples grow on a tall tree, and its leaves are deeply green both in winter and in summer. The fruit ripens in the middle of winter.

The orange is also a great fruit, golden-yellow in color, and the size of an apple like here at home. The core cools nicely,[325] but the peel does not do that. The orange ripens in the middle of winter, and throughout the year the old and the new fruit grow on the same tree. The leaves are evergreen.

The lime is a small fruit; it is the size of, and looks like, an egg and grows on shrubs. People make very good juice from it, after the consumption of which they always desire to enjoy it [even more]. Limes ripen also in winter and the bushes are evergreen.

Pistachios grow on a tree that has the same properties as the pear tree. The fruit is like a small hazelnut and has red skin. You find it available in all apothecaries. The princes and lords eat them after the meal [in the evening] during the fasting season; the tree is an evergreen.

Pharaoh figs[326] cannot be eaten; they grow on a tree that looks like a linden tree. That tree bears figs throughout the year. Those do not grow like other fruit next to the leaves, but directly on the hard wood.

Carob is a fruit in the shape of a pod. In this country [Outremer], the merchants who buy it in the countryside sell it here. They call it the Roman pod because when it becomes ripe, it tastes very sweet and they extract black honey from it.

Pepper grows on leafless rose bushes. The branches are deeply green. The pepper grows around the branches like peas, and it is white. When it is ripe, then the people scrape it off and place it in the sun, where it turns black. The bark [?] of the twigs is very bitter, but one makes a very good sauce from it. Some people say that they blacken the pepper with smoke with which the snakes are driven away. But that is not so because no one in that country who wants to put pepper into his food is so poor. It grows in the fields like other bushes, but when the pepper does not grow in the direction of the east and of the sun, then it is better and hotter.

Asparagus grows more than one span within one night and looks like hops. People eat it with oil. It breaks up a person's gall bladder stone and drives away all bladder illnesses that a person might have. When they let the asparagus grow for a long time, it develops thorns and thus becomes useless.[327]

Cotton grows in bundles on bushes; those are as tall as a man, and the leaves have holes like a cheese. Each bundle has four kernels/seeds, and around the kernel/seed, the cotton grows. Those kernels/seeds are sown in those countries, from which then grow bushes, and the people normally sow those bundles in the fields, as people do here with grain.

Rice has the same properties as wheat, but it grows in swampy countries; when it is ripe, people stomp on it in water, which makes its hulls come off. Then they let it rest in the sun, which makes it even more white.

Sugar cane[328] grows at the foot of mountains on plain fields next to flowing water. It grows in stalks and is called *Canamilla* [caramel].[329] Those stalks grow in a large area and reach the height of a man. They are much thicker than a thumb. There is much uncultivated land between those areas [i.e., they leave the field fallow].[330] In March, they chop down the stalks and put them in huge piles, cut into small pieces. Those they then grind with a millstone. Water/liquid oozes out which the people then simmer, which makes it thick and look like malt.[331] Then they pour that into a vat made out of brick stones, which is wide at the top and has a small hole at the side. That hole is stuffed shut with straw. Then they pour the brewing water into the vat which immediately becomes solid and hard. The liquid that oozes through the hole into the straw is honey. The substance in the middle is sugar, and that on the top is syrup, which the lords eat when they fast.

When the sugar cane is chopped down in March, they let much of the cane stand. They plant new ones in the soil, cover them with earth, and the plant is thus left located during the summer near the water. On Saint Lambertus Day[332] they place the stalks into the soil like a grape stock. Until March, as many new canes grow as there had been buds on the cane stalks. Those are then simmered again.[333] All that requires much effort and creates extensive work, but it also yields much money. The water that drives the millstone, which grinds the cane, has an extra use. It is, after all, a common custom in that land that when a man has a servant who is a good-for-nothing, then he sends him there [to the sugar mill]. He is thus forced to work throughout the day and night, and they give him nothing else as supplies but bread and water because the process of labor does not allow any break, and people pay close attention that everyone works well. Those [supervisors] give those who are good-for-nothing very hard blows and pay them no salary when they go home. There are at times two or three hundred of those who are good-for-nothing. The servant who has been there once then does what he can so that he does not have to go to that production site again.

There are three kinds of sugar in that country.[334] The first one which grows there is strong and black. They take it to the apothecary.

The other sugar that grows in the south of that country is red, and people add it to their food.

The third sugar, which grows more to the east, is white, and the further south it grows the better and whiter it is. There they sell sugar bread for a bezant.[335] Five half bezants make up a florin.[336]

In that country, there are three types of honey. The first one, people squeeze out of carob, and that honey is black.

The other type of honey is made out of sugar, and it is red.

The third type of honey originates from bees and is produced there just as here in our country, but it is much better and stronger.

A pomelo/grapefruit (bitter orange) is a fruit as large as two goose eggs, one upon the other, or smaller and larger, and yellow in color.[337] If you want to eat it, you have to peel it like an apple. It is so cold [sour] that you have to eat it with honey; otherwise, it cools a person too much on the inside.[338] That fruit mostly grows in the country that God had granted to the Jews when Joshua brought them there.[339] As soon as they had eaten the fruit, no more manna rained down from heaven.[340] For that reason, the Jews, wherever they live in the world, must have that fruit once a year. The tree on which it grows is green both in winter and in summer. The Jews who are poor collect that fruit to live on.

Galangal ginger and ordinary ginger grow as roots there, and the closer to India they can be found, the better and stronger they are.[341]

Incense oozes out of trees like lard. Those trees look like willows, and the incense comes out of them all the time and so thickly that it sticks together.

Thyme[342] grows on large plants that are like the ears of burned cereal, at which grow kernels of grain. Those plants stand together in large numbers, and when the plant is ripe, then people form a long row and bind many bands into them, pulling them through the plants. The thyme then gets stuck to the bands, and the people scrub it off and press it together like wax.

A small yellow fruit called nutmeg also grows there. It is very sweet, and it is very cheap, and many people from abroad die because they eat too much of it.

Many different kinds of tree fruit and plants grow there that are very common in that land and very rare here. I would have to say and write much about them.

On the other hand, there are many tree fruits and herbs on this side of the sea that are ubiquitous here and very rare there, such as cherries, Vistula cherries,[343] and hazelnuts, and also peas. Hence, people send those fruits as gifts to the lords and ladies there. Neither beech trees nor almond trees grow there.

Saffron does not grow in any country on this side of the sea except for in Aragon. People plant it in large fields, like small leeks. Each plant has a

Translation

flower at its head which is large and built like an autumn crocus, but it is white and blue, and each flower has three long fibers in its heart, which is the saffron. When it is ripe, the people break the flower and take the saffron out.

Here in this country the common broom grows,[344] which is enjoyed and appreciated throughout the world.[345] Merchants from Flanders import pots filled with soil into which small pieces of broom are planted. Those who can export them across the sea, sell them at a high price which they dictate. There is great demand over there among the lords, who like to look at the flower of the common broom. The poor people who cannot get a stalk collect flower petals from the broom, which the lords and the ladies make into perfume.[346] That perfume is much sought after in the apothecaries and very expensive. The same [poor] people bring to the [apothecaries] red berries, which cover the fields there, from which they make scarlet,[347] and with this trading good the people make a big profit. But not all people understand how to trade.

Herewith the book comes to an end.

May God grant us His holy peace.

COMMENTARY

1   Here and throughout, I follow Brall-Tuchel's use of new subheadings which help considerably to structure the entire text. Those, however, do not exist in the two manuscripts. They are all kept in bold which thus indicates the addition. Helmut Brall-Tuchel, *Von Christen, Juden und von Heiden: Der niederrheinische Orientbericht*, ed., trans., and commentary by Helmut Brall-Tuchel (2019). His contribution deserves great respect, and I would like to acknowledge his enormous accomplishment. The Middle Low German text is often not easy to understand, even for an expert of pre-modern German, so Brall-Tuchel's translation into modern standard German was a great help. Nevertheless, the original text contained in Ms. W*3, as edited by Anja Micklin (2021, see below) is the basis for this English translation, so I compared carefully how Brall-Tuchel had approached his task, which actually made it possible for me to offer numerous corrections throughout. Many times, I also had to disagree somewhat with the comments in his footnotes based on my own research. Rendering a Middle Low German narrative into modern English represents, to be sure, a very different challenge and charge.

The text has by now been edited critically by Anja Micklin, *Der »Niederrheinische Orientbericht«: Edition und sprachliche Untersuchung*. Rheinisches Archiv, 163 (Vienna, Weimar, and Cologne: Böhlau, 2021), which has allowed me to examine closely the original two manuscripts for the translation. Micklin offers mostly a historical-linguistic analysis but she is not concerned with the cultural-historical background and framework. See my review in *Mediaevistik* 35 (forthcoming). Cf. also my encyclopedia entry, "Anonymous: Niederrheinische Orientbericht [Low Rhenish Report about the Orient]" (1720 words), *The Literary Encyclopedia*. (https://www. litencyc.com/php/sworks.php?rec=true&UID=40912; last accessed on April 12, 2023). For the first edition of our text, accompanied with good background information, see Reinhold Röhricht and Heinrich Meisner, "Ein niederrheinischer Bericht über den Orient," *Zeitschrift für deutsche Philologie* 19 (1887): 1–86. As to the role of Egypt in this account, see Albrecht Classen, "Ägypten im *Niederrheinischen Orientbericht*: ein spätmittelalterlicher Augenzeuge," *Kairoer Germanistische Studien* 25 (2022): 15–27.

2   The author uses the phrase "und van allen landen van over mer" (30: and about all the lands across the sea), which scholarship has regularly called 'Outremer' after the French usage, referring to the four kingdoms set up in the Holy Land in the cause of the crusades. Those were the County of Edessa (1098–1150), the Principality of Antioch (1098–1287), the County of Tripoli (1102–1289), and the kingdom of Jerusalem (1099–1291). The kingdom of Jerusalem comprised modern-day Israel and Palestine, the West Bank, the Gaza Strip, and neighboring areas. This topic has already been covered by extensive historical research; for a helpful summary, see online at https://en.wikipedia.org/wiki/Crusader_states (last accessed on

Der Niederrheinische Orientbericht, *c.1350*

Oct. 16, 2022); cf. also, as one of many valuable studies, Nicholas Morton, *The Crusader States and Their Neighbours: A Military History, 1099–1187* (Oxford: Oxford University Press, 2020); Helena P. Schrader, *The Holy Land in the Era of the Crusades: Kingdoms at the Crossroads of Civilizations, 1100–1300* (Barnsley: Pen & Sword History, 2022).

3   In manuscript A (W261a), the sequence is different: about Christians, Pagans, and Jews. Out of respect for the Pagans (Muslims?), I capitalize that word throughout since the author refers to them as one religious community observing the Islamic faith. The scribes of both manuscripts are inconsistent in that regard, capitalizing only "Joeden" or "Joden" respectively, but not "kirstenen" or "krijsten" and "heiden."

4   Prester John was a famous mythical figure, allegedly a descendant of the Grail family who moved to India and established a Christian kingdom there dedicated to the Apostle Thomas. See the collection, *Prester John: The Legend and its Sources*, compiled and trans. by Keagan Brewer. Crusade Texts in Translation, 27 (Farnham: Ashgate, 2015); Ahmed Mohamed Abdelkawy Sheir, *The Prester John Legend Between East and West During the Crusades: Entangled Eastern-Latin Mythical Legacies*. Mediterranean Studies in Late Antiquity and the Middle Ages, 1 (Budapest: Trivent Publishing, 2022). On the Prester John legend, see Geraldine Heng, *The Invention of Race in the European Middle Ages* (Cambridge: Cambridge University Press, 2018), 363–73. Poets and writers throughout the entire Middle Ages were deeply familiar with him, at least with the nebulous personality, most likely a literary imagination and not a historically identifiable character. Prester John served exceedingly well for medieval Christians as a larger than life figure ruling in the East, a presumed fact which promised that Christianity could easily spread to and consolidate in that part of the world.

5   Brall-Tuchel, p. 31, note 4, discusses the various options of how to identify Tarsis, which could have been in Cilicia (today, southern Anatolia, or Turkey), or east of the Nile, or near the Red Sea, or in the "Third India," at least according to a contemporary of our anonymous writer, Johannes von Hildesheim. For this author, see Max Behland, *Die Dreikönigslegende des Johannes von Hildesheim: Untersuchungen zur niederrheinischen Übersetzung der Trierer Handschrift 1183/485 mit Textedition und vollständigen Wortformenverzeichnis* (Munich: Wilhelm Fink, 1968).

6   Also commonly identified as the Three Wise Men. Matthew 2 says only that they arrived from the East by following "His star." According to Acts 8:9 and Acts 13:6, they were wise men, perhaps leaders of their people, who practiced astronomy (or astrology) somewhere in the area of Babylon and were suddenly inspired by God to follow a star which would lead them to the promised king, God's son. Only later traditions identified the magi as a group of three men, i.e., kings, with specific names and skin colors. Their names, Melchior, Caspar, and Balthazar, were later inventions. We do not

even know whether they were kings, but the legend had a huge impact on their veneration, particularly in Cologne. Archbishop Rainald von Dassel brought a famous shrine to the cathedral in 1164; it allegedly contains the relics of the Three Holy Magi. This extraordinary shrine, certainly one of the largest medieval shrines, was created by the goldsmith Nikolaus von Verdun between 1190 and 1225. The relics used to be kept in Milan until the city was conquered and destroyed by Emperor Frederick II at the end of March 1162, who handed them over to Rainald as a gift on June 9, 1164. Those relics soon attracted streams of pilgrims to the cathedral in Cologne, which led to the foundation of a new building, the present cathedral, in 1248. Little wonder therefore that our author, most likely a citizen of Cologne, demonstrates such great interest in the history of the Three Holy Kings. See the excellent webpage, https://de.wikipedia.org/wiki/Dreik%C3%B6nigenschrein (last accessed on Oct. 25, 2022), which is accompanied by an extensive bibliography and good illustrations. For more recent research, see Manfred Becker-Huberti, *Die Heiligen Drei Könige: Geschichten, Legenden und Bräuche* (Cologne: Greven, 2005), and the contributors to the catalog accompanying the exhibition, *Die Heiligen Drei Könige: Mythos, Kunst und Kult: Katalog zur Ausstellung im Museum Schnütgen, Köln, 25. Oktober 2014 - 25. Januar 2015*, ed. Manuela Beer (Munich: Hirmer, 2014); *Reliquientranslation und Heiligenverehrung: Symposion zum 850jährigen Anniversarium der Dreikönigstranslation 1164; 24. Oktober 2014*, ed. Heinz Finger. Libelli Rhenani, 60 (Cologne: Erzbischöfliche Diözesan-und Dombibliothek, 2015). See also the excellent, well-illustrated catalog, *Balthazar: A Black African King in Medieval and Renaissance Art*, ed. Kristen Collins and Bryan C. Keene (Los Angeles, CA: J. Paul Getty Museum, 2023).

7   A region today in the southern part of the Caucasus, presently recognized by most countries as part of the nation of Georgia.

8   The adjectives 'strong' and 'weak', often used throughout the treatise, reflect the author's attitude toward various groups of Christians, 'strong' being reserved for full Catholics, i.e., western Christians; 'weak' for Orthodox and other Christians, i.e., eastern Christians, not strictly following the Catholic rules, having their own ecclesiastic structure, theological interpretations, liturgical customs, etc. See now these valuable new studies and editions/translations: *Invitation to Syriac Christianity. An Anthology*, ed. Michael Philip Penn, Scott Fitzgerald Johnson, Christine Shepardson, and Charles M. Stang (Oakland, CA: University of California Press, 2022); Françoise Briquel Chatonnet and Muriel Debié, *The Syriac World. In Search of a Forgotten Christianity*, trans. Jeffrey Haines (2017; New Haven, CT, and London: Yale University Press, 2023); *The Syriac World*, ed. Daniel King. The Routledge World (London and New York: Routledge, 2019).

9   The Maronites are a Christian sect living near Mount Lebanon in modern-day Lebanon following the preaching of Saint Maron, a

fourth-century Syrian hermit monk who converted the pagan people in the mountain region. They were able to maintain their religious independence and Greek and Syriac languages in the eastern Levant despite the strong presence of Islam well into the nineteenth century. Alternatively, the author might have had in mind Maniotes, or Mani, who lived in the southern Peloponnese, Greece; see https://en.wikipedia.org/wiki/Maniots (last accessed on Oct. 16, 2022).

10   It is not clear what Christian sects the anonymous had in mind here. Brall-Tuchel (p. 33) does not offer an opinion.

11   Prester John was a legendary, if not mythical, figure who allegedly brought Christianity to India and established an enormously powerful empire there. In the West, there was great hope that through his influence the Christian faith could be spread globally; cf. for instance, *Prester John: The Legend and Its Sources*, compiled and ed. Keagan Brewer (2015).

12   This could be "Sowa" or Saba in Saudi Arabia (south of Jeddah), or Soba in modern-day central Sudan, today only an archaeological site. The author appears to have drawn this information from Johannes von Hildesheim (c. 1310/1320–1375), one of his major sources, that is, from the *Historia Trium Regum* (History of the Three Kings, i.e., the Three Holy Magi). See John of Hildesheim, *The Three Kings of Cologne: An Early English Translation of the* Historia trium regum, ed. C. Horstmann (1886; Millwood, NY: Kraus, 1975); cf. also Max Behland, *Die Dreikönigslegende des Johannes von Hildesheim* (1968; see note 17).

13   This is a comment often made by other travelers as well, confirming that the use of paper money was already widespread in the Mongolian empire and in other Asian countries by the thirteenth century.

14   As in the case of Marco Polo, our author refers here to the earliest use of paper bills instead of coins as a currency.

15   Or: whom they all accept as the highest authority.

16   He probably means Saint Anthony of the Desert (c. 251–356), and not Saint Anthony of Padua. The former was a leader among the desert hermits and called 'Father of All Monks.' He was one of the first to move into the desert, where he was famously tempted by many seductive women, monsters, devils, and other creatures, a motif which artists throughout time have depicted in their work, such as Martin Schongauer and, following him, Michelangelo.

17   He was bishop of Jerusalem from 312 to shortly before 335. C. 325, he accompanied Helena Augusta, the mother of Constantine I, in her search at Jerusalem for relics of the Passion of Jesus, particularly the cross on which Jesus of Nazareth was thought to have been crucified. Bishop Athanasius praised Macarius as a role model in his battle against Bishop Arius. Both Athanasius and Arius fought heavily over the question of whether Christ was born as a human and then inspired with God's divinity (Arius)

Commentary

or whether He was born as God's son (Athanasius). The latter orientation defeated Arianism and is the dominant theology in the Christian Church.

18 "beissent" [Middle High German 'beizen'] – meaning, they go hunting with birds of prey, a noble sport practiced both in medieval Europe and the entire Middle East and beyond. It should be mentioned that many special birds of prey were imported from Iceland and Norway into Egypt and neighboring countries during the late Middle Ages. See now Thierry Buquet, "The Gyrfalcon in the Middle Ages: An Exotic Bird of Prey (Western Europe and Near East)," *Falconry in the Mediterranean Context During the Pre-Modern Era*, ed. Charles Burnett and Baudouin Van den Abeele. Bibliotheca Cynegetica, 9 (Geneva: Librarie Droz, 2021), 79–98.

19 Clearly, racial discrimination was already alive and well in the pre-modern world, but it is somewhat difficult to correlate it with modern forms of racism. Wolfram von Eschenbach, in his *Parzival* (c. 1205), has the protagonist's father Gahmuret comment that for him black people are ugly; but in the course of time, he changes his mind, falls in love with the black queen, Belakane, and has a son with her whose skin is black and white. See Andreas Mielke, *Nigra sum et Formosa: Afrikanerinnen in der deutschen Literatur des Mittelalters. Texte und Kontexte zum Bild des Afrikaners in der literarischen Imagologie*. Helfant Texte, T 11 (Stuttgart: helfant edition, 1992), 41–45. See now Albrecht Classen, "Blacks in the Middle Ages – What About Racism in the Past? Literary and Art-Historical Reflections," pre-print at https://www.qeios.com/read/KIJP54; comments at: https://www.qeios.com/notifications; *Current Research Journal of Social Sciences and Humanities* 6.1 (2023); online at: https://bit.ly/3MuEQsA.

20 The author does not realize his own contradiction here, first stereotyping them as ugly due to their skin color, and then praising them for their noble, elegant, and wealthy appearance.

21 While the original normally uses the verb 'to sing' for the ceremony of the Mass, there are various ways of saying it, either 'to read' or to 'to perform.' Subsequently, I will use interchangeable formulations.

22 It is not clear to what extent the author really understood the various languages he was exposed to, in order to be qualified to make this comment; it is certainly an expression of European hegemonic thinking, even in linguistic terms.

23 The Low-German term "wert" or "weert," etc. means island; there are still some family names like that today, such as the famous nineteenth-century Cologne poet Georg Weerth (1822–1856). There is also the toponym of "werth," such as in the case of Kaiserswerth near Düsseldorf. For the Middle High or Low German word "werder" for 'island,' see https://woerterbuchnetz.de/#0 (last accessed on Oct. 16, 2022).

24 Cattails and reed grass tend to grow in swamps. The former is occasionally called 'sausage tail' because of its oblong shape (in Latin, *Typha latifolia*). In German, due to its appearance, the cattail is facitiously identified as

"Kanonenputzer" (cannon cleaner). Reed grass is a generic term for a variety of grasses, such as the *Calamagrostis foliosa*, endemic to Northern California, or the *Calamagrostis ophitidis*, serpentine reedgrass that grows in bushes, and hence also in the Middle East.

25   He says, specifically, 'herbs' ("cruyt"), but he certainly means all kinds of plants.

26   Meaning crocodiles and other reptiles.

27   Probably the members of the various monastic orders and the mendicants.

28   This is all typical medieval monster lore and derived from the common late antique and early medieval sources widely available at that time, including the one-eyed cyclop or the siren.

29   Also known as Saint Thomas of India. He is known as the doubting apostle who did not want to believe that Christ had risen from the dead after His Passion until he witnessed Christ Himself and the wounds in His body (John 20:24–29). Later, he was said to have worked as a missionary in India after 52 C.E.

30   He means, as throughout, non-Catholic Christians, either Nestorians or Greek Orthodox Christians.

31   This geographical notion is derived from Gen. 2.10–14.

32   Nubia was the region along the Nile River situated between the first cataract of the Nile (just south of Aswan in southern Egypt) and the confluence of the Blue and White Niles (in Khartoum in central Sudan). It was the seat of one of the earliest civilizations of ancient Africa, the Kerma culture, which lasted from around 2500 B.C.E. until its conquest by the New Kingdom of Egypt under Pharaoh Thutmose I around 1500 B.C.E. See the useful overview on *Wikipedia* at https://en.wikipedia.org/wiki/Nubia (last accessed on Sept. 1, 2022), but there is no reference to Melchior as one of the Three Holy Magi. Their names are not mentioned in the Gospels; instead, those appear first in a Greek document from as late as c. 500 C.E. Melchior was traditionally associated with Persia, and not with Nubia, so we might wonder why our anonymous author confused this so much, unless he had another Nubia in mind.

33   Matthew 2:1–12; there are no comments on the Three Holy Magi in the other Gospels.

34   The kingdom of Chaldea existed in Babylonia, so present-day Iraq, again far away from where the anonymous wants to situate it.

35   Brall-Tuchel, in his note 23 (p. 41), refers to some historical events involving Frisian crusaders in Aachen, west of Cologne, in 1248, but the specifics of the reference to Frisian churches there remain elusive.

36   Here is one of the many typical linguistic problems. The original says literally: "They wear golden crowns of silver on their heads," which does not make good sense unless adapted as I have it here.

37   The tautology here is the author's own decision.

Commentary

38 The author here mingles a variety of traditions without paying any respect to historical or philological accuracy.

39 The author refers to the Muslims, as was customary at his time, as heathens. Here I use the correct term, Muslims.

40 Marco Polo, in chapter two of his *Travels*, trans. and with an intro. by Ronald Latham (London: Penguin, 1958), "The Road to Cathay," mentions that kingdom as well, 103: "When the traveller leaves Kan-chau, he journeys eastward for five days through a country haunted by spirits, whom he often hears talking in the night, till he reaches a kingdom called Erguuiul. This is subject to the Great Khan and forms part of the great province of Tangut, which comprises many kingdoms." See also Marco Polo, *The Travels of Marco Polo the Venetian*, with an intro. by John Masefield (1931; New Delhi: Chennai, 2003), online at https://books.google.com/books?id=AP7pPgFfyB4C&pg=PA135&lpg=PA135&dq=erginul&source=bl&ots=gslod5x-ug&sig=ACfU3U1EaGG1a4MPk3qdQv-l9euCbQ7IRuA&hl=en&sa=X&ved=2ahUKEwizuavqsPT5AhWYL0QIHUG7Dn4Q6AF6BAgVEAM#v=onepage&q=erginul&f=false, ch. LII, 135–36.

41 These Jacobites are not to be confused with the followers of the English King James II (Jacobus in Latin) after his expulsion in 1688 (that movement existed from 1688 until at least the 1750s). Instead, they were the followers of a certain Jacob (or James) Albardai, or Baradseus (or Zanzalus), who was appointed as bishop of Edessa in 541 and died in 578. They formed a Christian sect in Syria, Mesopotamia, and Babylonia, who subscribed to the Monophysite doctrine. According to that doctrine, Jesus Christ's nature always remained divine despite His human life cycle, whereas the Council of Chalcedon in 451 had established that He had two natures, human and divine, which became the standard doctrine of the Western Church and the critical theological issue separating it from the Eastern Orthodox Church until today. See Sidney Griffith, "'Melkites', 'Jacobites' and the Christological Controversies in Arabic in Third/Ninth-Century Syria," *Syrian Christians under Islam, the First Thousand Years*, ed. David Thomas (Leiden and Boston: Brill, 2001), 9–55; online at: https://brill.com/display/book/9789004497467/B9789004497467_s004.xml

42 The anniversary of the foundation of the church. Alternative terms are "Kirmes," "Kirchfest," or "Kermesse." In modern parlance, this is simply a type of folk festival celebrated all over the German-speaking lands with food, drinks, and dance, usually no longer associated with a Church festival, except in Catholic regions.

43 Probably Abyssinians, in northern Ethiopia, also called Habesha, whereas the Muslims in the highlands to the south are called Tigre, among other tribal names.

44 It was fairly common in the Middle Ages to equate, or rather confuse, Babylon with Cairo.

Der Niederrheinische Orientbericht, c.1350

45   This is a most important reference to the Jewish pogroms in the Rhineland and particularly in Cologne. Brall-Tuchel, note 36, associates it with the Black Death and the pogrom in Cologne in 1349. In 1327, rumors were already spreading about so-called 'evil things' allegedly found in the courtyard of the synagogue and in the communal well. The city council, however, promised the Jews its strong protection. In 1340, the choir in the cathedral was decorated with derogatory images attacking Jews. Also, the expansion of the Jewish quarter was forbidden. In the summer of 1348, Strassburg (Strasbourg) merchants living in Cologne colported the rumor that the Jews had instigated Christians in their own town to poison the wells. At that time, the Black Death spread rapidly all over Germany, and so also in Cologne, but the city council was greatly concerned for the Jewish citizens, at least officially, and sent out numerous messengers to inquire about situations in other cities. In the summer of 1349, refugees from other cities reported that Jews had been murdered elsewhere. The Jews in Cologne subsequently secured more weapons to defend themselves, while the city council threatened anyone with the death penalty if they dared to attack Jews, but this was all to no avail. on the night of August 23 to 24, 1349, a mob stormed the Jewish quarter, slew its population, among them four rabbis, and pillaged the apartments. Four houses caught fire and burned down. The murdering and pillaging continued for weeks. Even the synagogue was burned down, and the ground underneath was dug up because people believed that they would find treasure. Although the members of the city council had decided numerous times to declare that the Jews would be safe under their watch, in the end they were helpless, if they were not secret co-conspirators in the pogrom. In 1350, the archbishop and the city negotiated and agreed on splitting the Jewish property left over from the pogrom, a rather callous reaping of profits after all those hypocritical promulgations. See the monumental collection of relevant sources for virtually all major towns and cities in the Holy Roman Empire, *Germanica Judaica*, ed. Zvi Avneri. Vol. II: *Von 1238 bis zur Mitte des 14. Jahrhunderts* (Tübingen: J. C. B. Mohr, 1968), 433. Significantly, there were no reports about any pogroms in Aachen, west of Cologne, ibid., 1–2, which underscores that our anonymous most probably originated from Cologne. It is difficult to understand why he dated the pogrom in 1341 in correlation with the events in Cologne; maybe he had already lived for so many years in the Middle East that he could not remember some of the details from events back home. Or he referred here to the event in Ethiopia – or rather in Egypt – that happened in 1341, whereas the pogrom in Cologne took place in 1349, simply building historical correlations. That would indicate that the anonymous wrote his treatise after 1349, maybe around 1355. The mix of tenses in this passage makes it hard to decide on the actual situation. For an overview, see Christoph Cluse, "Juden am Niederrhein während des Mittelalters: Eine Bilanz," *Jüdisches Leben im*

Rheinland: Vom Mittelalter bis zur Gegenwart, ed. Monika Grübel and Georg Mölich (Cologne, Weimar, and Vienna: Böhlau, 2005), 1–27.

46 https://www.newadvent.org/cathen/09683b.htm; https://en.wikipedia.org/wiki/Maroneia (both last accessed on Sept. 1, 2022).

47 This group was considered heretical by the mainstream Church because they subscribed to ritual forms of sexual activities and used cult prostitutes. According to Revelation (2:6), Christ had rejected them already.

48 He probably means a small amount of money, enough to buy some bread.

49 He uses the term "in orienten" in a rather limited fashion, emphasizing thereby only the Middle East, maybe up to the Black Sea.

50 The Frisians are found today on the northern coast of the North Sea up to Denmark and beyond. Between the tenth and the thirteenth centuries, the Frisians enjoyed a considerable degree of independence from the Dutch/Hollandic dukes, but in 1422 Dutch troops conquered Western Frisia and set up a new military class in Central and Eastern Frisia, mostly subjugating the ordinary people. See Carl Woebcken, *Das Land der Friesen und seine Geschichte* (1932; Walluf b. Wiesbaden: Sändig, 1973); Thomas Steensen, *Die Friesen: Menschen am Meer* (Kiel and Hamburg: Wachholtz, 2020). See the excellent historical overview of the Frisians' freedom until the fourteenth century online at https://de.wikipedia.org/wiki/Friesische_Freiheit (with a good bibliography).

51 Saint Anthony of Padua: 1195–1231; Saint Macarius of Jerusalem I: bishop of Jerusalem from 312 to shortly before 335 C.E.

52 Both manuscripts use the same spelling, "Abcas" (256–57), but Brall-Tuchel has wrongly copied "Abtas" and translates it rather inexplicably as "Abchasien" (p. 49).

53 The author drew extensively from the famous chronicle about Armenia by the Armenian prince Hayton; see https://gallica.bnf.fr/ark:/12148/btv1b6000425w/f15.item; Bibliothèque nationale de France, Département des manuscrits, NAF 886; for a text edition, see *La flor des estoires de la terre d'Orient*, ed. Charles Kohler, *Recueil des historiens des croisades*. Documents arméniens, 2 (Paris: Imprimerie nationale, 1906), Vol. 2. See now *Die Geschichte der Mongolen des Hethum von Korykos (1307) in der Rückübersetzung durch Jean le Long "Traitiez des estas et des conditions de quatorze royaumes de Aise" (1351): kritische Edition mit parallelem Abdruck des lateinischen Manuskripts Wrocław, Biblioteka Uniwersytecka, R 262*, ed. Sven Dörper. Europäische Hochschulschriften, 13, 236 (Frankfurt a. M., Bern, et al.: Peter Lang, 1998).

54 This nebulous country is mentioned in numerous sources consulted by our anonymous, such as Johannes von Hildesheim, Hethum of Karykos, Marco Polo, and John of Mandeville.

55 In the Middle Ages, scientists still believed in the geocentric worldview, meaning that the earth was stable and that the sun circled around it. Scientists such as Tycho Brahe, Johannes Kepler, and Galileo Galilei only

discovered in the sixteenth and seventeenth centuries that the opposite is the case (heliocentric paradigm).

56 He means, of course, that the fog blinded the Muslims and served as a protective cover for the Christians.

57 In a subordinate clause, the author comments that no one has ever left the fog who had entered it before, which is contradictory to the previous statement.

58 He probably refers here to the ancient empire of Alexander the Great.

59 It is unclear what pope he had in mind here. It might have been Innocent V, who followed Pope Gregory X on January 21, 1276, for a few months (until June 22). He had participated in the Second Ecumenical Council in Lyon in 1274 and endeavored to broker a peace treatise between Constantinople and King Charles I of Naples, but Charles was only interested in military conquest, and then Innocent V passed away. Alternatively, the anonymous might have had in mind Pope Innocent VI (1352–1362) who had also tried but failed to negotiate with the Byzantine emperor John V Palaeologus but that seems to have been too late for the overall report. As to the Council in Lyon, see https://en.wikipedia.org/wiki/Second_Council_of_Lyon (last accessed on Sept. 4, 2022). The anonymous must have heard all kinds of rumors coming from Europe, but he was apparently not quite sure about the details. If he composed the account only after his return, he did not bother to verify this passage.

60 The following sentence specifies that he is referring only to male criminals, as if women were not liable or responsible for any wrongdoing.

61 This is a generic expression for a long prison term.

62 The alb is the priest's long vestment worn during Mass. It comes down to the ankles and is white, hence the name, 'alb,' from Latin 'albus' (dull or matt white).

63 Saint Sergius and Saint Bacchus were fourth-century Roman Christian military officers in Galerius's army and were subsequently revered as martyrs and military saints by the Catholic, Eastern Orthodox and Oriental Orthodox Churches. Both had secretly converted to Christianity, and refused, once exposed, to abandon their new faith. As a consequence, they were brutally abused, tortured, and then killed. Oddly, Brall-Tuchel, p. 57, note 46, along with his source, Anna-Dorothee von den Brincken, *Die 'Nationes Christianorum Orientalium' im Verständnis der lateinischen Historiographie von der Mitte des 12. bis in die zweite Hälfte des 14. Jahrhunderts.* Kölner historische Abhandlungen, 22 (Cologne and Vienna: Böhlau, 1973), 369–79, refer to a completely different saint who was said to have been Mohammed's teacher. This does not seem to make sense in the current context.

64 Pope John XXII (1316–1334). He was born as Jacques Duèze (or d'Euse) and was the second longest serving pope in Avignon, Provence. For a

respectable biography, see, for instance, https://www.newadvent.org/cathen/08431a.htm (last accessed on Dec. 13, 2022).

65   This was Leo V, the last king of the Armenian kingdom of Cilicia (1320–1341). For the latest research on Cilicia, see now Arabella Cortese, *Cilicia as Sacred Landscape in Late Antiquity: A Journey on the Trail of Apostles, Martyrs and Local Saints*. Spätantike – Frühes Christentum – Byzanz, 53. Reihe B: Studien und Perspektiven (Wiesbaden: Reichert Verlag, 2022).

66   This was probably King Philipp VI de Valois, 1293–1350.

67   Again, an important internal reference to the anonymous's personal background associated with the Lower Rhineland.

68   Tarsis, Tharsis, or Tharshish was a mythical city, mentioned a number of times in the Bible and other texts, allegedly situated in the vicinity of modern-day Lebanon and Israel. The author implies that major parts of that city lie in rubble, but it still existed in his time. The following comments, however, indicate that he might have meant the city of Tarsus in ancient Cilicia, which was located in the modern-day province of Mersin, southern Turkey, west of Adana. See https://www.worldhistory.org/Tarsus/ (last accessed on Sept. 5, 2022).

69   This was Pope Benedict XII (1334–1342).

70   Another chronological reference that allows us to date this text more precisely, that is, *post quem* 1349 when the Christian population of Cologne committed a pogrom against the Jewish community.

71   Literally in the original: to send many hardships into his hands.

72   This is the so-called Hundred Years' War between England and France, 1337–1451. We can use the beginning of that war as a *terminus post quem* for the dating for our text, but it remains a rather vague reference since the author was aware of many historical events and knew many facts from earlier times.

73   Again, this reference allows us to date the text more specifically because it addresses only the initial defeats of the French.

74   Brall, 61, n. 52, states that dukes with that name could not be identified. The source clearly says "kynck" (269), and since the following paragraph already talks about Cilicia, I suspect that the scribe contracted that name somehow. See the contributions to *Rough Cilicia: New Historical and Archaeological Approaches: Proceedings of an International Conference held at Lincoln, Nebraska, October 2007*, ed. Michael C. Hoff and Rhys F. Townsend (Oxford: Oxbow Books, 2013).

75   Cilicia is a former kingdom and now a geographic region in southern Anatolia, today Turkey; it was ruled by the Armenian kingdom during the time of the First Crusade from 1096 to 1099, and became a military and economic stronghold for the crusaders until the end of the thirteenth century. After King Levon V's death in 1342, John of Lusignan (dynasty on Cyprus) was crowned king as Gosdantin IV, but since he tried to impose the rule of the Roman Catholic Church, he quickly alienated the local

population. In 1375, Cilicia was taken over by the Egyptian Mamluks, the Bahri dynasty under Al-Mansur Ala' ad-Din Ali ibn Sha'ban ibn Husayn ibn Muhammad ibn Qalawun (1368–May 19, 1381), better known as al-Mansur Ali II (ruled from 1377–1381). By 1342, after the death of King Levon V, internecine strife and religious conflicts had already deeply undermined and destroyed the internal cohesion and paved the way for the kingdom's collapse. There are numerous references to Cilicia in the New Testament, see for example Acts 15:23, Acts 21:39, or Galatians 1:21.

76 This means, as in most other cases at European courts, two or more guests tended to share one dish, or vessel with food.

77 Another example of some contradictory reporting because the seeds are supposed to be planted and not to be collected.

78 Research has not yet been able to determine what people the anonymous author might have had in mind; one strong possibility is that they were Sinti or Roma, nomadic people who had originated from India, had then lived in Egypt, and reached Europe in the early Middle Ages. But they could have been other nomadic people as well. See Brall-Tuchel, p. 65, n. 54.

79 Manuscript A (W261a) might contain a mistake here since the text (271) specifically says, if a woman finds her husband with another man: "yren man bij eyme anderen manne." It seems highly unlikely that the author might have implied cases of homosexuality among those people. After all, 'sodomy' or the 'unmentionable sin' was regarded as one of the worst sins a Christian could commit. For a comprehensive and annotated bibliography on this intriguing topic, see now Albrecht Classen, "Queer Medieval," *Oxford Bibliographies in Literary and Critical Theory*, ed. Eugene O'Brien (New York: Oxford University Press, Sept. 22, 2021); online at: https://www.oxfordbibliographies.com/view/document/obo-9780190221911/obo-9780190221911-0111.xml?rskey=2ZgQVg&result=6&q=Queer#firstMatch (last accessed on June 9, 2023).

80 Above, the scribe used the term 'village,' but here it is 'city,' or 'town.'

81 Here I deviate specifically from the source and do not use the modern term 'Muslim,' as I have done above, as complex as the religious culture of the medieval Persians might have been. For the role of Persia in medieval literature, see Albrecht Classen, "The Topic of Persia in Medieval Literary Imagination, with a Focus on Middle High German Literature," *Ceræ: An Australasian Journal of Medieval and Early Modern Studies* 8 (2021; appeared in 2022): 35–65; https://ceraejournal.com/wp-content/uploads/2022/07/Vol-8-FULL-VOLUME.pdf. At the end of section One, our author briefly returns to the issue of the Persians, adding further details about that country and culture.

82 The various Jewish groups mentioned by the anonymous are not clearly or correctly identified by Brall-Tuchel, p. 67 (no note given). He simply renders the original names as found in the text and does not realize that "Osey" are the Essenes.

Commentary

83   This is the historical biblical name for the land bordering Judea to the south and Galilee to the north, hence in the central part of Palestine. According to the ancient historian Josephus (first century C.E.), the Mediterranean was its western, and the Jordan River its eastern, border.

84   Jeroboam I was the first king of the northern kingdom of Israel; he is roughly dated as having ruled in the early eighth century B.C.E., see 1 Kings, Exodus 32:1–10, and 1 Corinthians 12:28–30.

85   See Mark 12:18 and John 11:47–50.

86   Before, it was clear that the anonymous had previously had the Essenes in mind, whereas here he seems to confuse them with the Assassins, who had nothing to do with Jews but were a special group of Muslim terrorists (literally) operating under the rule of the Old Man from the Mountain in an area that is today northeast of Teheran; see now Albrecht Classen, "Assassins, the Crusades, and the Old Man from the Mountains in Medieval Literature: With an Emphasis on The Stricker's *Daniel von dem Blühenden Tal*," *Marginal Figures in the Global Middle Ages and the Renaissance*, ed. Meg Lota Brown. Arizona Studies in the Middle Ages and the Renaissance, 47 (Turnhout: Brepols, 2021), 123–40. Brall-Tuchel, p. 69, note 60, refers to that terrorist group, which was historically well known as operating in secret and quite effectively until the rule of the Old Man from the Mountains was destroyed by the Mongols.

87   The anonymous has not much to say about the various tribes of Jews, and offers more historical, i.e., biblical, comments than personal observations. Overall, he does not express any particularly negative views of Jews.

88   Again, the anonymous always talks about 'heathens' ("Heiden") when he means 'Muslims,' surely a pejorative term.

89   It is uncertain what people or religious group the anonymous might have had in mind. A search online did not yield anything, except a reference to an online version of our entire text, edited by L. Ennen, "Der Orient: Ein Bericht vom Niederrhein aus dem Ende des 14. Jahrhunderts," *Orient und Occident insbesondere in ihren gegenseitigen Beziehungen: Forschungen und Mittheilungen*, ed. Theodor Benfey (Göttingen: Dieterich, 1862), 449–80, and 627–46; online at: https://books.google.com/books?id=Hy0JAAAAQAAJ&pg=PA466&lpg=PA466&dq=Agartini&source=bl&ots=sZFFfIOwiC&sig=ACfU3U0dv0hKC0PqcyttuOZ-rRdsP4HsEJA&hl=en&sa=X&ved=2ahUKEwiymbW7-ob6AhU7LU-QIHeizAHMQ6AF6BAgbEAM#v=onepage&q=Agartini&f=false   (last accessed on Sept. 8, 2022).

90   The anonymous switches between "Ysmahelite[s]" (275, or 125r) and "Ysmahelis" (276).

91   The Byzantine Emperor Flavius Heraclius ruled from 610 to 641; hence in Constantinople, since Rome, i.e., the western Roman empire, had already fallen to the East Roman general Odoacerin in 476.

Der Niederrheinische Orientbericht, *c.1350*

92 The original clearly says: as much as he wanted; Brall-Tuchel translated (in my translation): "as much as he demanded."

93 He means, of course, the prophet Mohammed. Throughout, the anonymous uses the spelling "Magomet" or "Machomet," which I replicate here, at the risk of confusion, to stay faithful to the source.

94 There are many cities with the name of 'Antioch,' but it can only have been a city in the area of the eastern Mediterranean; see https://en.wikipedia.org/wiki/Antiochia (last accessed on Sept. 8, 2022). The original text says literally: "he moved with the entire country and the power."

95 The anonymous labels it *Alkoranius*.

96 We cannot expect the anonymous, definitely not a university-trained individual, to have studied Islam objectively or even to know the fundamentals of the Qur'an, and this despite the fact that he lived in the Middle East for many years. In a way, here we face the standard notions about the Muslims' faith, as was probably common among lay people in the West with a fairly low degree of education. See John V. Tolan, *Sons of Ishmael: Muslims Through European Eyes in the Middle Ages* (2008; Gainesville, Tallahassee, et al., FL: University Press of Florida, 2013); and the contributions to *Western Views of Islam in Medieval and Early Modern Europe: Perception of Other*, ed. Michael Frassetto and David A. Blanks (1999; New York: Palgrave Macmillan, 2016); *Medieval Latin Lives of Muhammad*, ed. and trans. Julian Yolles and Jessica Weiss (Cambridge, MA: Harvard University Press, 2018). See also John Tolan, Gilles Veinstein, and Henry Laurens, *Europe and the Islamic World: A History*, trans. by Jane Marie Todd (Princeton, NJ, and Oxford: Princeton University Press, 2013).

97 Again, there are differences in the spelling of Mohammed or Muhammed, sometimes as 'Magometz,' sometimes as 'Machomet,' but most commonly, as noted above, as 'Magomet.' See also Edeltraut Klueting, "*Quis fuerit Machometus?* Mohammed im lateinischen Mittelalter (11.–13. Jahrhundert," *Archiv für Kulturgeschichte* 90 (2008): 283–306; John V. Tolan, *Faces of Muhammad: Western Perceptions of the Prophet of Islam from the Middle Ages to Today* (Princeton, NJ: Princeton University Press, 2019).

98 Literally, he says "also lustich," meaning: 'so much filled with fun.'

99 He means the 'minaret.'

100 Literally, the author says that they 'fall down,' but 'kneel down' is more appropriate.

101 The word 'mosque' is not used here for a long time, only 'kirche' for 'church.' The word 'mosque' appears only a little later.

102 Generally, Muslims pray in the direction (*qibla*) of the Kaaba in Mecca. Originally, they prayed in the direction of Jerusalem but after the Kaaba was identified by God as the holy site in several verses of the Qur'an revealed to Muhammad in the second Hijri year, the *qibla* was changed. Today, if the precise direction (*ayn al-ka'bah*) cannot be determined, the general direction (*jihat al-ka'bah*) is accepted. Again, our anonymous is

Commentary

not very clear about these Muslim customs and might not have observed them carefully.

103 The anonymous uses the phrase "mysschida" (281, or 126r) for 'mosque,' which is actually fairly close as a transcription.

104 In other words, he celebrates it as his birthday.

105 The phrase 'cutting into two pieces' is repeated several times and can thus be regarded as a customary formulation for the death penalty by the sword.

106 The Mongols besieged and conquered Baghdad in 1258, after which the city declined significantly in economic, political, and educational terms. Only after Iraq had gained its independence from the British kingdom in 1932 did Baghdad again grow in importance.

107 As to the correct spelling, see "A qāḍī (Arabic: قاضي, romanized: Qāḍī; otherwise transliterated as qazi, cadi, kadi, or kazi) is the magistrate or judge of a sharī'a court, who also exercises extrajudicial functions, such as mediation, guardianship over orphans and minors, and supervision and auditing of public works," quoted from https://en.wikipedia.org/wiki/Qadi (last accessed on Oct. 16, 2022).

108 In practical terms, the qāḍī was the central judicial figure, running the legal court system as a judge. During the Abbasid Caliphate, the rank of 'chief qāḍī' was established, in charge of maintaining law and order, peace and justice. Here I use the spelling preferred by our author.

109 The author uses two equivalent terms for the same kind of person, "Begarde" and "Clusener." From the thirteenth century or so, lay women (beguines) and lay men (beghards) formed pious communities particularly in North-western Europe. Their members did not take religious vows and could leave at any time, but they were spiritually committed to each other and lived in spiritual isolation from the rest of the urban community. Those lay women and lay men pursued a life of contemplative prayer and active service in the world, earning their living by their own hands (often, textile work). The Church viewed those lay people with considerable distrust, and many secular writers ridiculed them as pseudo-religious. In particular, in the late Middle Ages, beguines were often identified as secret prostitutes, a vicious malignment of those devout people, who were really *mulieres religiosae* (religious women). The Church Council of Vienne (1311–1313) even condemned beguines as heretics, but this did not seem to have had a significant impact on this movement, which prospered considerably well into the fifteenth century. The beguinage in Bruges, for instance, has been one of the most famous until the present day, but similar communities can be found all over modern-day Belgium (Ghent, Brussels, Mechelen), France (Cambrai, Valenciennes, Liège), The Netherlands (Amsterdam, Breda, Utrecht), and northwest Germany (Neuss, Cologne, but then also Lübeck and Brunswick). It is difficult to imagine what the anonymous might have observed in the Middle East when he transfers this unique

term for lay brothers to the Muslim world. See Walter Simons, *Cities of Ladies: Beguine Communities in the Medieval Low Countries, 1200–1565.* The Middle Ages Series (Philadelphia: University of Pennsylvania Press, 2001); Frank-Michael Reichstein, *Das Beginenwesen in Deutschland. Studien und Katalog.* Wissenschaftliche Schriftenreihe Geschichte. Band 9. 2nd ed. (Berlin: Verlag Dr. Köster, 2017); Tanya Stabler Miller, *The Beguines of Medieval Paris: Gender, Patronage, and Spiritual Authority* (Philadelphia, PA: University of Pennsylvania Press, 2014); most recently, eadem, "'More Useful in the Salvation of Others': Beguines, *Religio*, and the *Cura Mulierum* at the Early Sorbonne," *Between Orders and Heresy: Rethinking Medieval Religious Movements*, ed. Jennifer Kolpacoff Deane and Anne E. Lester (Toronto, Buffalo, and London: University of Toronto Press, 2022), 214–41. See also John Van Engen, *Sisters and Brothers of the Common Life: The Devotio moderna and the World of the Later Middle Ages.* The Middle Ages Series (Philadelphia, PA: University of Pennsylvania Press, 2008). The large number of critical studies on the beguines, above all, indicates the fact that historical research has recognized how much this religious lay movement played a major role at its time, undermining in many different ways the patriarchal authority of the Catholic Church, though not in any radical or militant fashion.

110 It is not quite clear what differences there might be between beguines and religious women. Moreover, the term 'beguine' normally refers only to a religious movement by women in Northwestern Europe. Our author simply transfers terms he was familiar with to the world in Egypt and elsewhere.

111 Oblates were members of monasteries who had joined at a very early age, even as children; their parents hoped to gain God's grace thereby, especially when they had several children and only one could inherit the estate. The psychological problems for those oblates, who were never exposed to the realities outside the monastery, must have been tremendous. Oblates were typical of Christian monasticism at least until the thirteenth century, after which the various Orders began to refuse to accept such young people as members of their communities as it was, ultimately, a huge burden and responsibility. It might be doubtful that the anonymous really observed Muslim oblates; instead, he most likely transferred this phenomenon to the Islamic world which he wanted to describe in parallel terms, so that his Low German audience could understand his report better, as imaginative as it might have been, at least in this case. The term 'oblate' derives from the Latin verb 'offerre,' 'to offer' or 'to hand over,' that is, to pass on or to dedicate their own child to God. Rule no. 59 of the Rules of Benedict specifies the institution of oblates, or 'oblatio puerorum.' See Pater Bruno Rieder, "Oblaten des Klosters Disentis," online at: https:// www.kloster-disentis.ch/fileadmin/pdf/bkd22/Oblaten_Beschreibung. pdf (last accessed on Sept. 13, 2022). See also A. Rüther, "Oblate," *Lexikon*

des Mittelalters vol. VI: *Lukasbilder bis Plantagenêt* (Munich and Zürich: Artemis & Winkler Verlag, 1993), 1336–37; Maria Lahaye-Geusen, *Das Opfer der Kinder: ein Beitrag zur Liturgie-und Sozialgeschichte des Mönchtums im Hohen Mittelalter*. Münsteraner theologische Abhandlungen, 13 (Altenberge: Oros-Verlag, 1991); Roberta Werner, *Reaching for God: The Benedictine Oblate Way of Life* (Collegeville, MN: Liturgical Press, 2013).

112 This comment confirms what I noted above, that is, the pervasive distrust by the male clergy of the beguines, particularly as deceivers and cheaters, or even worse, as prostitutes.

113 Below, the author explains that many pilgrims get voluntarily blinded so that they no longer can/must see the physical world.

114 Lambert's feast day is September 17, cf. H. Grotefend, *Taschenbuch der Zeitrechnung des deutschen Mittelalters und der Neuzeit*. 11th ed., ed. Th. Ulrich (Hanover: Hahnsche Buchhandlung, 1971), 73. Lambert of Maastricht, or Saint Lembert (c. 636–c. 705), was bishop of Maastricht-Liège (Tongeren) and died as a martyr for having denounced King Pepin's affair with Alpaida, mother of the later Charles Martel, the founder of the Carolingian dynasty. For good background information, see the German lexicon of saints, online at https://www.heiligenlexikon.de/BiographienL/Lambert_von_Maastricht.html (last accessed on Sept. 14, 2022).

115 In contrast to previous evidence closely associating the anonymous with Cologne, here he seems to affiliate himself with Aachen. Most likely he was connected to both cities, which are not far apart in any case.

116 This is probably supposed to be Baghdad. The distance between Baghdad and Mecca today consists of 1,399 kilometers or 869 miles. Divided by twenty-five days, this would then mean 34.8 miles per day.

117 He means the Bedouins who have traditionally inhabited the regions of the Arabian Peninsula, North Africa, the Levant, and Mesopotamia. For historical perspectives, see James Moreton Wakeley, *At the Origins of Islam: Muḥammad, the Community of the Qurʾān, and the Transformation of the Bedouin World* (Oxford, Bern, Berlin, et al.: Peter Lang, 2022). See also the contributions to *Die Beduinen: Stammesgesellschaften und Nomadismus im Nahen Osten. Akten des I. Symposiums der Max Freiherr von Oppenheim-Stiftung, 17.–18. März 2016 im Rautenstrauch-Joest-Museum, Köln*, ed. Gernot Wilhelm. Max-Freiherr-von-Oppenheim-Stiftung: Schriften der Max-Freiherr-von-Oppenheim-Stiftung, 19 (Wiesbaden: Harrassowitz, 2018).

118 This could refer to Pope Benedict XI (pope from 1303 to 1304), or to Pope Benedict XII (pope from 1334 to 1342), unless, though rather unlikely, the anonymous had a much earlier Pope Benedict in mind.

119 It is not clear whether the anonymous author intends to ridicule these confessions; the text in the original indicates some criticism: "altze luckerlichen" (Brall-Tuchel, p. 80; too quickly, or superficially). To be more accurate, however, the manuscripts have "alze lutlijchen" (W261a, p. 288,

36r) or "altze lutterlichen" (W*3, p. 289, 128r). Both here and throughout, there are notable differences between Brall-Tuchel's edition and the critical edition by Micklin.

120 The anonymous writer seems to combine traditional Christian concepts of Mohammed, personal observations, rumors, and stereotypes about the founder of Islam.

121 This means literally that they subject themselves to a gouging out of their eyes.

122 Al-Aqsa Mosque or Jami' Al-Aqsa; this is the Dome of the Rock located on the Temple Mount in the Old City of Jerusalem, a site also known to Muslims as the al-Haram al-Sharif or the Al-Aqsa Compound. The Dome is the oldest work of Muslim architecture, built between 691 and 692; it collapsed in 1015 and was rebuilt in 1022–1023.

123 Genesis 28:10–19.

124 Genesis 32: 23–33.

125 Genesis 14:18–20.

126 2 Samuel 6:8.

127 Luke 2:22–24.

128 Luke 2: 25–29.

129 Luke 2: 41–52.

130 It is not quite clear what the logical connection between the temperatures during the day and the need to bring for oneself the necessary bedding and utensils might be. But it is very likely that the anonymous author appears to reflect here his own experiences as a traveler and guest in local taverns or guest houses.

131 Although only a fleeting reference, the anonymous writer provides an important clue as to the practice of toleration (not necessarily tolerance) in the Muslim world; for the same notion in medieval (Christian) Europe, see Albrecht Classen, *Toleration and Tolerance in Medieval and Early Modern European Literature*. Routledge Studies in Medieval Literature and Culture, 8 (New York and London: Routledge, 2018; paperback, 2021); and id., *Religious Toleration in the Middle Ages and Early Modern Age: An Anthology of Literary, Theological, and Philosophical Texts* (Berlin: Peter Lang, 2020).

132 He refers here to the outbreak of the Black Death, which began among the Muslim population a few years earlier than in medieval Europe (1347). See, for instance, John Aberth, *The Black Death: The Great Mortality of 1348–1350: A Brief History with Documents* (Boston, MA: Bedford/St. Martin's, 2005); Ole J. Benedictow, *The Complete History of the Black Death* (Woodbridge, Suffolk: The Boydell Press, 2021). For the history of the Black Death in the Muslim world, see now Michael Walters Dols, *The Black Death in the Middle East* (Princeton, NJ: Princeton University Press, 2019). For the latest medical-historical research, particularly on the spread of the Black Death from Mongolia across the Himalayas down to India

and from there to the Black Sea, and then to the western hemisphere and Arabia, see the contributions to *Pandemic Disease in the Medieval World: Rethinking the Black Death*, ed. Monica H. Green (Kalamazoo, MI: Arc Medieval Press, 2015).

133 Literally the text says, 'they stayed as they were.' This means that they abandoned their hope that conversion to Christianity might help them avoid God's wrath since the plague was considered to be its result. It is rather ironic that the author deconstructs from the start all concepts of a certain faith as a guarantee against a medical epidemic. In the face of such a catastrophic plague, no faith, i.e., no religion, could help. We could also draw a relevant analogy to the current Covid-19 plague which raged across the world in 2020 and 2021 and continues to linger at the time when I composed this comment (Sept. 2023).

134 He probably means individual composers of travelogues, either aristocrats or friars.

135 Melek is a Turkish name of Arabic origin, meaning 'angel' for girls and 'king' for boys. The anonymous, however, might have heard the pronunciation of 'Malik,' 'Melik,' or 'Melekh,' meaning 'king' in Arabic. The female version is 'Malikah' meaning 'queen.'

136 As stated above, in the Middle Ages western authors regularly but erroneously equated Baghdad with Babylon as that was the famous city mentioned in the Old Testament (Tower of Babel, Genesis 11). But the ancient site of Babylon is situated just south of Baghdad, today the capital of Iraq. Most famously, King Nebuchadnezzar ruled over Babylon and fought against the Jews, see 2 Kings 17–25 and 2 Chronicles 32–36. See also Jeremiah 21:4–10.

137 It is not clear from the text what the difference between Suria and Syria might be; the author probably thought of the northern part of the country, which was a district, as a separate kingdom. In the mid seventh century, the Umayyad dynasty took over Syria and divided it into the four regions of Damascus, Homs, Palestine, and Jordan. In 750, the Abbasid dynasty replaced the previous government as a result of its internal collapse and moved the capital from Damascus to Baghdad.

138 This was a confederation of cities in the southeastern Levant, such as Ashdod, Ashkelon, Ekron, Gath, Gaza, and for a time, also Jaffa.

139 His real name was Al-Ashraf Salāh ad-Dīn Khalil ibn Qalawūn, 1290–1293. But from 1285, the name of "al-Malik al-Ashraf" was added, as a term of endearment, and our anonymous author could only try to reproduce the Arabic word, mangling the original rather badly. However, here we recognize once again how familiar he must have been with the historical sources and also the Arabic language since, with some fantasy, "Sapheraff" is not that far away from "al-Ashraf."

140 His full name was Al-Malik an-Nasir Nasir ad-Din Muhammad ibn Qalawun (1285–1341). He ruled as the ninth Bahri Mamluk Sultan of Egypt

on three occasions: December 1293–December 1294, 1299–1309, and 1310 until his death in 1341. At the end of the first time he was deposed, and at the end of the second time he abdicated the throne. See online at https://en.wikipedia.org/wiki/Al-Nasir_Muhammad (last accessed on Sept. 18, 2022). There are, so it seems, no contemporary Arabic sources telling us anything about the Sultan's physical appearance. My colleague, Prof. Emad Aboghazi at Cairo University, comments in an email (Jan. 27, 2023): "I do not think that the descriptions you refer to apply to Muhammad ibn Qalawun." This would strengthen the claim that our anonymous author referred to a later Sultan.

141 He uses the telling phrase, "perlement" (W*3, p. 299) or 'parliament,' a meeting of people to discuss issues, as in the modern-day 'Parliament,' or 'Congress.'

142 He refers to the Arabic name, "Alkair."

143 This refers to Saint Margaret of Antioch; her feast day was July 13 (today it is July 20), and in the Orthodox Church it is July 17. She was said to promise extraordinary indulgence for those who wrote or read her *Life* or pleaded for her help. She was martyred in 304 during the Diocletian persecutions of Christians.

144 It is unclear whether he also means people having been trained, maybe as acrobats.

145 Vespers is one of the seven canonical hours, usually held at dusk. During the canonical hours, which structured the daily lives in monasteries, monks or nuns were supposed to pray. Benedict of Nursia (480–547), in his deeply influential monastic rules, drew primarily from biblical texts to explain the canonical hours, Psalm 118/119:164, "Seven times a day I praise you,", and Psalm 118/119:62, "At midnight I rise to praise you." This so-called Divine Office consisted of: Matins (nighttime), Lauds (early morning), Prime (first hour of daylight), Terce (third hour), Sext (noon), Nones (ninth hour), Vespers (sunset evening), and Compline (end of the day). Matins, Lauds, and Vespers were the main hours, the others were the minor hours. The prayers were included in the so-called breviary, a literary genre on its own, somewhat related to the late medieval Book of Hours, normally composed for secular ladies and others, who used it to perform their daily ritual in the privacy of their homes, mostly beautifully illustrated.

146 The author uses the term "zoldener," which could mean 'soldiers' or rather mercenaries. What is really implied here are the Mamluks, the slave soldiers of Turkic, Caucasian, Eastern, and Southeastern European origin, taken prisoner during the various war campaigns and who, after having served in the military for a long time, were finally set free without being fully exempted from their bondage. In the course of time, the Mamluks rose in power and eventually took over the rule of Egypt, even though their status was still identified as that of slaves, during the Mamluk Sultanate (1250–1517). Ultimately, the Mamluks were most responsible

Commentary

for the final defeat of the Christian crusaders and the fall of Acre in 1291. See, for instance, David Ayalon, *Outsiders in the Lands of Islam: Mamluks, Mongols and Eunuchs*. Collected Studies Series, 269 (London: Variorum Repr., 1988); Daniel Pipes, *Slave Soldiers and Islam: The Genesis of a Military System* (New Haven, CT: Yale University Press, 1981); *The Mamluks in Egyptian Politics and Society*, ed. Thomas Philipp and Ulrich Haarmann. Cambridge Studies in Islamic Civilization (Cambridge: Cambridge University Press, 1998); Robert Irwin, *Mamluks and Crusaders: Men of the Sword and Men of the Pen* (Farnham: Ashgate, 2010). For an excellent overview, see also https://en.wikipedia.org/wiki/Mamluk (with an extensive bibliography and good illustrations).

147 Brall-Tuchel, in his translation, rendered "wapen" as 'weapons,' but 'coats of arms' [wappen] seems to make more sense.

148 I added this phrase as an explanation for the water since they would certainly not have drunk the water before having been seated at the dinner table.

149 These were obviously the various diplomats who had been charged with attending the Sultan's court.

150 All these details support the claim that the anonymous author must have actually visited Egypt, indeed, and might have been an actual eyewitness, and this is very different from the later armchair author, John Mandeville.

151 The entire process proves to be highly ritual, with each person present fully aware of his official role in the individual steps of the consumption of food, certainly a public affair of great significance. For medieval European history, see, above all, Gerd Althoff, *Die Macht der Rituale: Symbolik und Herrschaft im Mittelalter* (Darmstadt: Primus Verlag, 2003).

152 This is a remarkable comment, "myt gemache," which signals, according to the anonymous author, that the festive dinner was carried out calmly and without stress, with each person knowing well his status and hence the sequence of the individual steps in the food preparation and serving of the food.

153 Since this took place in Egypt, hence in a Muslim culture, no alcohol was consumed.

154 The author repeatedly states that people from all over the world were in attendance, which could mean many different things. Undoubtedly, at the Cairo court, there were representatives of many countries located in the Near or Middle East, but probably not from the West, though we cannot exclude this. The collective term implies, to be sure, a sense of globalism within the Muslim world, as observed and reflected by the anonymous writer. Cf. Albrecht Classen, "Global History in the Middle Ages: A Medieval and an Early Modern Perspective. The *Niederrheinische Orientbericht* (c. 1350) and Adam Olearius's *Vermehrte New Beschreibung der Muscowitischen vnd Persischen Reyse* (1647; 1656)," *Philological Quarterly* 100.2 (2021): 101–34.

Der Niederrheinische Orientbericht, c.1350

155 Perhaps, the dinner table was folded together, as the original implies, which says, literally: 'Once the tables had been lifted.'

156 Both in medieval Europe and the Arabian world, hunting with birds of prey and greyhounds was greatly enjoyed and regarded as the most noble sport. In medieval European literature, the falcon often represented courtly love itself since the wild animal had to be tamed and trained. Different kinds of falcons were actually often imported from northern Europe to the Islamic courts. However, hunting with those birds has also been popular in the Far East, such as in the Altai Mountains between Kazakhstan and China. See Thierry Buquet, "The Gyrfalcon in the Middle Ages: An Exotic Bird of Prey (Western Europe and Near East)," *Falconry in the Mediterranean Context During the Pre-Modern Era*, ed. Charles Burnett and Baudouin Van den Abeele. Bibliotheca Cynegetica, 9 (Geneva: Librarie Droz, 2021), 79–98; here 97; id., "Aspects matériels du don d'animaux exotiquess dans les échanges diplomatiques," *Culture matérielle et contacts diplomatiques entre l'occident latin, Byzance et l'Orient islamique (XIe–XVI s.): Actes du colloque de Liège, 27–28 avril 2015*, ed. Frédéric Bauden. Islamic History and Civilization (Leiden and Boston: Brill, 2021), 177–202; online at: DOI: https://doi.org/10.1163/9789004465381_009. Cf. also N. Mehler, "The Export of Gyrfalcons from Iceland During the 16th Century: A Boundless Business in a Proto-Globalized World," *Raptor and Human: Falconry and Bird Symbolism Throughout the Millennia on a Global Scale*, ed. K.-H. Gersmann and O. Grimme. Advanced Studies on the Archaeology and History of Hunting, 1.1 (Kiel and Hamburg: Wachholtz, 2018), vol. 3, 995–1020.

157 For more details, see https://en.wikipedia.org/wiki/Falconry_training_and_technique#Jesses (last accessed on Sept. 26, 2022).

158 Again, the anonymous author probably means the countries to the east, and not in Europe; still, here we recognize, once again, the global perspective pursued by the Sultan and fully understood by the author.

159 He uses really only this mild expression, "leiff hadde" (liked them), and does not talk about 'love' in the erotic sense of the word.

160 Meaning, those who were part of their own courts.

161 Literally, litters held by two horses or more. A palanquin was more typical of Asia, where a litter or coach is carried by two people. Another term would be sedan chair.

162 Brall-Tuchel oddly translated here: 'above the floor.'

163 This was December 26. According to Brall-Tuchel, that wedding between the Sultan and the daughter of the governor of Damascus, Seif al-Din Tengiz, had taken place a decade earlier. He has no explanation for that chronological inconsistency and is puzzled about the anonymous author's lack of historical accuracy. I was not able to identify this governor in biographical-historical terms. The official title her father held, if this is the correct historical figure, was Viceroy of Syria. She married the Sultan

Commentary

al[n]-Nasir Muhammad in 1337. But the 1340s saw a series of rulers ascending to the throne, then died either a natural death or were assassinated and replaced by another descendent of al-Nasir Muhammadr (r. 1310–1341) and his Tatar wife, Kuda. His seventh son, Al-Nasir Badr ad-Din Hasan ibn Muhammad ibn Qalawun (1334/35–17 March 1361), better known as al-Nasir Hasan (in some spellings: an-Nasir Hasan), conceived by a concubine wife, reigned twice in 1347–1351 (deposed in favor of one of his younger brothers) and 1354–1361 when he was assassinated by one of his own Mamluks, Yalbugha al-Umari. He married Tulubiyya (d. 1363), a daughter of one of his father's emirs, Abdullah an-Nasiri. In my opinion, our author really referred to Al-Nasir Badr ad-Din Hasan as the one whose wedding he observed, since this would coincide most closely with the comments by our anonymous author. Nevertheless, this is a very complicated dynastic history. See P. M. Holt, "Al Nāṣir Muḥammad," *The Encyclopedia of Islam*. New Edition, ed. C. E. Bosworth, E. van Donzel, et al. Vol. VII (Leiden and New York: E. J. Brill, 1993), 991–993. For a study of an-Nasir Muhammad, see Amalia Levanoni, *A Turning Point in Mamluk History: The Third Reign of Al-Nāṣir Muḥammad Ibn Qalāwūn (1310–1341)*. Islamic History and Civilization, 10 (Leiden and Boston: Brill, 1995). As to his building program in Cairo, and that of other sultans, see Jim Antoniou, *Historical Cairo: A Walk Through the Islamic City* (Cairo: The American University in Cairo Press, 1998), 105–07. This can be complemented by André Raymond, *Arabic Cities in the Ottoman Period: Cairo, Syria and the Maghreb*. Variorum Collected Studies Series (Aldershot, Hampshire, and Burlington, VT: Ashgate, 2002), 150–57. He also identifies the period from 1341 to 1412 as "an era of crises that reached its height with the reigns of al-Nāṣir Faraj (1399–1412)" (148). For a genealogy of the entire dynasty, see http://mamluk.uchicago.edu/qalawunids/qalawunid-pedigree.pdf (last accessed on Sept. 29, 2022). See also the contributions to *Making Cairo Medieval*, ed. Nezar AlSayyad, Irene A. Biermann, and Nasser Rabbat. Transnational Perspectives on Space and Place (Lanham, MD: Lexington Books, 2005). I believe, hence, that this reference to the sultan's wedding was historically correct and does not contradict the other historical comments, and this contrary to Brall-Tuchel's assumption that the author got confused or combined various aspects of Mamluk history. Altogether, including the references to the Black Death and to the pogrom against Jews in Cologne, this strongly suggest that our anonymous writer composed his treatise well after 1347, perhaps in the middle of the 1350s. However, according to Emad Aboghazi, "two of the sons of Sultan al-Nasir Muhammad ibn Qalawun married a daughter of a prince called Tengiz, but I'm not sure if he's the same person (the governor of Damascus) or not. In the beginning, Sultan Al-Kamil Shaaban married her, and after his death, his brother Sultan Haji married her, that was about 1347" (email from Jan. 26, 2023). Prof. Aboghazi also comments: "it is certain that

Sultan al-Nasir Muhammad ibn Qalawun married the daughter of the governor of Damascus Tengiz. In 1338 she bore him his son Saleh, who later became a sultan."

164 The original wording is confusing; it says, literally, "the sultan took his best woman in marriage."

165 Burning of wheat was probably a measure to have good smells for the festivities. For the author (and for us) this was a clear sign of decadence and excessive wastefulness.

166 Again, here we find yet another example of the extraordinary degree of toleration practiced at the Sultan's court.

167 The author suddenly switches to the present tense here.

168 Again, this is the evening prayer according to the Divine Office. In the original Middle Low German text, the phrase is "complet," which is still the same in modern German, "Complet."

169 Again, a switch in tense.

170 He probably means ibises and not cranes, but I leave that word here because it is his common phrase. The ibis is a long-legged wading bird which can also fly. Our author could probably not distinguish between cranes and ibises. As we will see later, his ornithological comprehension was not the best since he often mixes facts with myths about birds and also animals, a phenomenon not untypical of his time.

171 It is unclear whether the sultan greeted only those on one side and his son those on the other side, or whether the sultan acknowledged everyone.

172 The reference to the 'people' is qualified here to indicate all of his soldiers or mercenaries.

173 Despite the generic term 'people' used here, the text is only seemingly unspecific: "hie weder komen ynder syn banner" (p. 317, fol. 135r) because this is all part of the military organization.

174 It deserves mentioning, of course, that hunting with falcons, or any other birds of prey, implied that the bird was trained to fly off the falconer's gloved fist, chase a bird and kill it, let it drop, and return to its master, landing on the glove. The master would then feed it as a reward.

175 There are many possibilities as to what kind of eagles that might have been: white-tailed eagle, lesser fish eagle, white-bellied fish eagle, the white-headed eagle, etc.

176 For a general introduction to this type of falcon, see https://en.wikipedia.org/wiki/Gyrfalcon, which is good enough for our purposes (last accessed on Sept. 30, 2022).

177 These ornithological details underscore the author's meticulous observations about the art of falconry as practiced in Egypt and also his personal interest in this special art of hunting. This suggests again his noble status because he was apparently familiar with this aristocratic sport.

178 It is a little unclear what the author means here. The text specifies that no one was supposed to start a fight, but maybe he intended to say that no

one was allowed to oppose the Sultan's wish to return home. Both here and throughout, we observe the extent to which the political and cultural situation at the Sultan's court is described as being highly peaceful, joyful, and tolerant.

179 This might have been an early form of polo as a military exercise and game. It is commonly assumed that polo as a sport originated in Persia c. 2000 years ago, then was copied in India, where it then appealed to the British colonialists in the nineteenth century: the birthdate, so to speak, of modern polo. See, for instance, https://www.rulesofsport.com/sports/polo.html, or https://www.historic-uk.com/CultureUK/The-Origins-of-Polo/ (both last accessed on Sept. 30, 2022). There is clear evidence that numerous nomadic tribes in Central Asia were already playing forms of polo in the sixth century B.C.E., and the Kurdish Sultan Saladin (twelfth century) was said to have been an expert polo player. See Horace A. Laffaye, *The Polo Encyclopedia*. 2nd ed. (2004; Jefferson, NC: McFarlane, 2015). Our source proves to be critical in the assessment of where and when polo was played, especially in Egypt. The author's detailed explanations indicate, however, that polo was not known in Europe, given his explicit comments about how this sport was practiced.

180 Those were mostly papal statements regarding legal and administrative matters concerning the Church in response to inquiries or court discussions.

181 Of course, he expected the enemy's surrender and only offered a peaceful surrender instead of a military onslaught.

182 The author paints a very impressive picture of the Sultan as a wise, yet also resolute military commander who first tried to achieve his goal in a peaceful fashion, but once all his offers had been turned down, became relentless, and finally crushed his enemies. The castle, however, was not damaged; instead, it served him for his own public glory.

183 Monks could not leave their monasteries, whereas friars such as the Franciscans and Dominicans were free to move around, especially because their tasks were to preach (the former) and teach (the latter). Thus, it is most likely that the anonymous author meant the second group.

184 Brall-Tuchel (p. 113, note 90) assumes that the Sultan mentioned here was an-Nasir Muhammadr (r. 1310–1341), which would imply that those political and military unrests began in 1335. The better option would be, as I have already indicated above, An-Nasir Badr ad-Din Hasan ibn Muhammad ibn Qalawun (1334/35–17 March 1361), also known as an-Nasir Hasan, which would hence take us to 1355. Online we learn, to extend my comments from above: "An-Nasir Hasan was killed by one of his own *mamluks*, Yalbugha al-Umari, who headed a faction opposed to an-Nasir Hasan's elevation of the *awlad al-nas*" (Wikipedia, https://en.wikipedia.org/wiki/An-Nasir_Hasan, last accessed on Sept. 30, 2022). See also Frédéric Bauden, "The Sons of al-Nāṣir Muḥammad and the Politics of Puppets: Where Did It

All Start?," *Mamluk Studies Review* (Middle East Documentation Center, The University of Chicago) 13.1 (2009): 53–81; online at https://knowledge. uchicago.edu/record/1153?ln=en. If that is correct, we would have to date the *Niederrheinische Orientbericht* somewhat later than previous scholarship has assumed, that is, as late as c. 1356 or 1360.

185 The narrative voice shifts quickly, which makes it a little confusing for us, so I have slightly adapted the syntax to help clarify the various perspectives pursed here.

186 This is the Monastery of the Temptation near Jericho, the earliest structures erected by the Byzantines in the sixth century C.E. above the cave traditionally claimed to be the site where Jesus spent forty days and forty nights fasting and meditating during the temptation of Satan. Christ's temptation was recorded three times in the New Testament, Matthew 4:1–11, Mark 1:12–13, and Luke 4:1–13.

187 Brall Tuchel, p. 113, note 92, identifies him as Seif al-Din Tengiz (the correct version would be, at least in an English transcription: Sayf ad-Din Tankiz ibn Abdullah al-Husami an-Nasiri, who was the viceroy of Syria from 1312 to 1340 during the reign of the Bahri Mamluk Sultan an-Nasir Muhammad, cf. https://en.wikipedia.org/wiki/Tankiz [last accessed on Sept. 30, 2022]). This would not, however, correspond with our previous observations. I suggest looking for another historical figure with a similar name, unless we acknowledge that the anonymous author was confused and merged various characters from different periods to fit into his narrative. Sayf ad-Din Tankiz was followed by Yilbugha an-Nasiri (1340–1350), Sayf ad-Din Manjak (1350), and others, but there are gaps in our knowledge. For a chronological list of the so-called Mamluk na'ibs, see https:// en.wikipedia.org/wiki/List_of_rulers_of_Damascus#Ayyubid_emirs_ (some_were_also_sultans_of_Egypt) (last accessed on Sept. 30, 2022).

188 He might refer here to the war between King Alfonso XI, who was assisted by a fleet of the kingdom of Aragon and a fleet of the Republic of Genoa, against the Muslim-held city of Al-Jazeera Al-Khadra, called Algeciras by Christians, located near the Straits of Gibraltar. The city fell on March 26, 1344, and was incorporated into the kingdom of Castile. This was the first military engagement by Europeans during which gunpowder was used. We know, however, also of a Queen Elizabeth of Sicily (1298–1352), who was involved in serious internecine strife, especially after her husband Peter II's death in 1342. Her four-year-old son Louis was crowned as the future king, while her brother-in-law, Duke John, acted as regent until his death from the plague in 1348. At that time, Elizabeth took over the regency until her death around 1350 or 1352. For the very complicated dynastic politics under her and for the numerous conflicts in Sicily at that time, see https://en.wikipedia.org/wiki/Elizabeth_of_Carinthia,_Queen_of_ Sicily (last accessed on Oct. 18, 2022). Our author, however, tells a rather different story, perhaps rather fanciful. According to Reinhold Röhricht

and Heinrich Meisner, "Ein niederrheinischer Bericht über den Orient" (1887): 1–86; here 48, note 8, the author basically made up this historical account. Brall-Tuchel, p. 115, n. 93, by contrast, suggests that the author had in mind Sancia of Majorca (c. 1281–July 28, 1345), Queen of Naples from 1309 until 1343 as the wife of Robert the Wise. After his death in 1343, she took over the regency for her step-granddaughter, Joanna I of Naples, until 1344. However, her biography does not fit with the account provided by our author either. For a critical study, see Ronald G. Musto, *Queen Sancia of Naples (1281–1345) and the Spiritual Franciscans in Women of the Medieval World* (Oxford: Basil Blackwell, 1985); Adrian S. Hoch, "Sovereignty and Closure in Trecento Naples: Images of Queen Sancia, alias 'Sister Clare'," *Arte medievale / Istituto della Enciclopedia Italiana* (Milan) 2. Ser. 10.1 (1997): 121–39; Matthew J. Clear, "Piety and Patronage in the Mediterranean: Sancia of Majorca (1286–1345), Queen of Sicily, Provence and Jerusalem," Ph.D. diss., Falmer, University of Sussex, 2000. What is puzzling here is the author's rather detailed discussion of this war, the visit by the queen of Sicily to Cairo, her further travels, and the Sultan's decision not to get involved in that war.

189 This is a reference to Byzantine Emperor Heraclius (c. 575–Feb. 11, 641), who was involved in many battles, both against the Persians, who at first had almost crushed him, and then the Muslims. After having gained much territory to the east, he then lost most of it to the Muslim forces of the Rashidun Caliphate, especially in the Battle of Yarmouk in 636. Heraclius enjoyed great respect, not only as a military leader, but also for his attempts at establishing religious harmony within his Byzantine empire. Ultimately, he failed in that, but he succeeded in returning the True Cross, one of the holiest Christian relics, to Jerusalem. For Heraclius, see, for instance, Walter E. Kaegi, *Heraclius: Emperor of Byzantium* (Cambridge: Cambridge University Press, 2003); James Howard-Johnston, *Last Great War of Antiquity* (Oxford: Oxford University Press, 2021), and Nikolas Hächler, "Heraclius Constantine III – Emperor of Byzantium (613–641)," *Byzantinische Zeitschrift* 115.1 (2022): 69–116. Brall-Tuchel, p. 117, n. 94, associates this reference with the literary legend of Eraclius, best formulated by Gautier d'Arras in his late twelfth-century French romance *Eracle*, which was later adapted by the Middle High German poet Meister Otte (early thirteenth century). Specifics about the historical figure and the literary manifestation are not given here, so the reference to "Eraclius van Cosdras" (116) represents a superficial form of name dropping, indicating, however, that the poet had some literary training, or at least exposure. See Karen Pratt, "The Genre of Gautier d'Arras's Eracle: A Twelfth-century French 'History' of a Byzantine Emperor," *Reading Medieval Studies* XXXIV (2008):169–90; online at: https://www.reading.ac.uk/gcms/-/media/project/functions/research/graduate-centre-for-medieval-studies/documents/rms200811-k-pratt-the-genre-of-gautier-darrass-eracle.

Der Niederrheinische Orientbericht, *c.1350*

pdf?la=en&hash=F262D48710A6618D949716E3CDBDBCF8; eadem, Karen Pratt, *Meister Otte's Eraclius as an Adaptation of Eracle by Gautier d'Arras*. Göppinger Arbeiten zur Germanistik, 392 (Göppingen: Kümmerle Verlag, 1987). See also her edition, Gautier d'Arras, *Eracle*, ed. and trans. by Karen Pratt. King's College London Medieval Studies, XXI (London: King's College London; Centre for Late Antique & Medieval Studies, 2007).

190 An apostate is someone who has renounced his/her faith without having necessarily adopted a new one. An apostate is an abhorrence to any religious organization, both Christianity and Islam, and so also Judaism, etc. because s/he questions the foundations of the specific religion altogether.

191 The tense of this sentence is unclear. The narrator only says: "als hie de Joden" (329, fol. 138v), which could be translated as "as it happens to the Jews here" or as "as it happened to the Jews here."

192 May 13. He was born in Armenia, was the bishop of Tongere, Belgium, and died in Maastricht.

193 Brall-Tuchel, p. 119, note 98, assumes that the author meant Cairo, but there is no reason to claim that. After all, the sultan had traveled to Damascus and would not have suddenly returned to Cairo.

194 She was an early Christian martyr and said to have been Saint Peter's spiritual daughter. Her feast day is May 31.

195 This is a generic term medieval Christian authors preferred to use for all those whom they did not accept into their fold or simply did not understand. Reinhold Röhricht and Heinrich Meisner, "Ein niederrheinischer Bericht über den Orient" (1887), 50, note 8, suspect that the anonymous author might refer here to the Druze people populating the Levant, such as modern-day Lebanon and Syria. They are not Muslims, but adhere to a syncretic form of religion, relying on the teachings of Hamza ibn Ali ibn Ahmad and ancient Greek philosophers like Plato, Aristotle, Pythagoras, and Zeno of Citium. See Cyril Roussel, *Les Druzes de Syrie*. Contemporain publications, 31 (Beirut: Presses de l'Ifpo, 2011); Abbas Halabi, *The Druze: A New Cultural and Historical Appreciation* (Reading: Ithaca Press, 2015).

196 Brall-Tuchel, p. 121, notes 203–08, offers the identification of the modern city names. The anonymous author does not realize the contradiction in his account, having first emphasized that there are no major cities in Turkey, and now listing many significant cities.

197 Geoffrey of Bouillon (1060–1100) was the major leader in the First Crusade and briefly ruled Jerusalem from 1099 to 1100, refusing, however, to take on the title of king; instead, he called himself 'Advocate of the Holy Sepulchre.' Our author here draws from early crusading history, following a pattern of mixing different time periods in his account.

198 The discovery of the holy lance, or the Lance of Longinus, that pierced the side of Christ when he was hanging on the cross (John 19:34), was attributed to St. Helena, Empress and mother of the Roman Emperor

Constantine (r. 306–336), when she went on a pilgrimage to the Holy Land in 326 C.E. to atone for her son's sins against his own family. For a good overview and especially illustrations, see https://www.liturgica-lartsjournal.com/2022/09/the-empress-helena-and-finding-of-true.html (last accessed on July 15, 2023). For a solid scholarly study, see Stephan Borgehammar, *How the Holy Cross Was Found: From Event to Medieval Legend*; with an appendix of texts. Bibliotheca theologiae practicae, 47 (Stockholm: Almqvist&Wiksell, 1991). See also Antonina Harbus, *Helena of Britain in Medieval Legend* (Woodbridge, Suffolk, and Rochester, NY: Brewer, 2002).

199 This is modern-day Antalya, located on the southwest coast of Anatolia, bordering the Taurus mountains. Its history goes back to the Romans, but it was originally settled in c. 200 B.C.E.

200 This is today's Tortosa on the Syrian Mediterranean coast, the second largest Syrian harbor after Latakia.

201 Ephesus dates back to the tenth century and flourished considerably during the Roman time. Today, it is particularly famous for Saint Paul addressing the Ephesians in one of his letters, Ephesians 1:3–6. John the Evangelist was said to have died in Ephesus. Saint Helena erected a church above his grave.

202 The author uses the term "koufhuys" (p. 335, fol. 140r), meaning 'merchants' house' or 'store.'

203 He refers here to the Hundred Years' War between England and France, generally dated as lasting from c. 1337 to c. 1451 and longer. The issue pertained to the privilege of ruling over the kingdom of France which various generations of English kings claimed for themselves. Both sides developed new war technologies and fighting strategies during the entire long-term war campaign. Ultimately, King Edward IV of England abandoned any further attempts to fight against the French in the Treaty of Picquigny in 1475. Our author here confirms that he was fully aware of the contemporary historical and military events in western Europe.

204 See the comments by Brall-Tuchel (p. 125, n. 116), who identifies this Zabalin, Zablin, or Jalabi as Sasa Bey, a Turkish warlord of the Menteşoğulları principality, who conquered Ephesus on October 24, 1304. Contrary to the terms of the treaty of surrender, the Turks pillaged the church of St. John and deported most of the local population to Thyrea, Greece. The majority of the remaining Christians were slaughtered. Shortly thereafter, Ephesus was ceded to the Aydinid principality that stationed a powerful navy in the harbor of Ayasuluğ (the present-day Selçuk, next to Ephesus). Cf. Andreas Külzer, "Ephesos in byzantinischer Zeit: ein historischer Überblick," *Byzanz – das Römerreich im Mittelalter*. Part 2.2: *Schauplätze: Byzantium – the Roman Empire in the Middle Ages*, ed. Falko Daim and Jörg Drauschke. Römisch-Germanisches Zentralmuseum: Monographien, 84 (Mainz: Römisch-Germanisches Zentralmuseum, 2011), 31–49;

Clive Foss, *Ephesus After Antiquity: A Late Antique, Byzantine, and Turkish City* (Cambridge: Cambridge University Press, 1979).

205 Here we face yet another example of the global situation in the eastern Mediterranean as clearly described by the author. Our anonymous writer observed everything surprisingly calmly, as if this was nothing extraordinary.

206 It is not clear whether he wanted to identify the Turks in those negative terms, or whether he committed yet another syntactical error combining different aspects quite loosely.

207 Brall-Tuchel, p. 125, n. 118, identifies this outbreak with 1347. If that is correct, his previous dating regarding the Sultan and some of his emirs would have to be changed as well.

208 The Hagia Sophia was the main Greek Orthodox church in Constantinople, built by the eastern Roman emperor Justinian I as the Christian cathedral of Constantinople between 532 and 537. Well into the early sixteenth century, it was considered to be the largest Christian church. After the fall of Constantinople in 1453, it was converted into a mosque by Mehmed the Conqueror and became the principal mosque of Istanbul until the 1616 construction of the Sultan Ahmed Mosque. It was closed in 1931 and reopened in 1935 as a museum under the secular Republic of Turkey. Recently, on July 10, 2020, the Hagia Sophia was reclassified as a mosque upon the initiative of the Turkish President Recep Tayyip Erdoğan as part of his efforts to re-Islamize Turkey. Of course, the modern history does not concern us here. There is much literature on the Hagia Sophia; see, for instance, W. Eugene Kleinbauer and Anthony White, *Hagia Sophia* (London: Scala Publishers, 2007); İlhan Akşit, *The History and Architecture of the Hagia Sophia*, trans. Stuart Kline (Istanbul: Akşit Kültür Turizm Sanat Ajans, 2014).

209 Marie Favereau, *The Horde: How the Mongols Changed the World* (Cambridge, MA, and London: The Belknap Press of Harvard University Press, 2021); for a useful timeline of Mongol history, see also https://en.wikipedia.org/wiki/Timeline_of_the_Mongol_Empire#1260s (last accessed on Oct. 3, 2022). The year 1268, however, does not seem to have been a time of particularly dangerous threats for the Near East and the eastern Mediterranean. For the most recent research, see Johan Elverskog, *The Precious Summary: A History of the Mongols from Chinggis Khan to the Qing Dynasty* (New York: Columbia University Press, 2023).

210 Here I prefer to stick to the term 'heathen' because it is not certain that the author means 'Muslims,' as he normally does when he discusses the Arabic world. To stay close to our source, I do not refer to those people as 'Mongols,' as would be correct, but as 'Tatars' since that was the common practice in most or even all western medieval sources.

Commentary

211 Although the text does not say so here, the author clearly implies that the representatives of the various faiths were allowed to preach, a clear case of publicly practiced tolerance.

212 https://en.wikipedia.org/wiki/Lord%27s_Prayer (last accessed on March 3, 2023). This site offers the various versions next to each other and discusses the philological history of this famous prayer.

213 This is a highly curious phenomenon because the friars treat the children almost like slaves, in a very un-Christian fashion. Cf. the contributions to *Slavery and the Slave Trade in the Eastern Mediterranean (c. 1000–1500 CE)*, ed. Reuven Amitai and Christoph Cluse. Mediterranean Nexus 1100–1700, 5 (Turnhout: Brepols, 2018); Hannah Barker, *That Most Precious Merchandise: The Mediterranean Trade in Black Sea Slaves, 1260–1500*. The Middle Ages Series (Philadelphia, PA: University of Pennsylvania Press, 2019); Albrecht Classen, *Freedom, Imprisonment, and Slavery in the Pre-Modern World: Cultural-Historical, Social-Literary, and Theoretical Reflections*. Fundamentals of Medieval and Early Modern Culture, 25 (Berlin and Boston: Walter de Gruyter, 2021); *Incarceration and Slavery in the Middle Ages and Early Modern Age: A Cultural-Historical Investigation of the Dark Side in the Pre-Modern World*, ed. Albrecht Classen. Studies in Medieval Literature (Lanham, Boulder, New York, and London: Lexington Books, 2021). The role of orphan children and others as slaves, however, has not been adequately covered, and especially not this section in the *Niederrheinische Orientbericht* as rather unusual textual evidence for this phenomenon.

214 This is a typical syntactical lapse by the author, who really means whenever they besiege a country or a castle.

215 He means, of course, shooting with bows and arrows.

216 In other words, he observes a bit of economic competition and notes that the Sultan looked out for his own people. However, the author does not say at all that the Christian merchants were unwelcome or blocked from reaching the Mongol territories.

217 The term 'Cathay' was commonly applied by Central and Western Asians and Europeans to northern China, hence to a separate country, including Mongolia. Giovanni da Pian del Carpine (c. 1250), William of Rubruck (c. 1293), Marco Polo (c. 1300), or Odorico da Pordenone (c. 1320), among many other travel writers (such as the Florentine merchant Francesco Balducci Pegolotti [c. 1340] and the armchair traveler John Mandeville [c. 1370]), relied on that word as well, so it is no surprise that our anonymous author followed their example, whether he knew their texts or not. See Donald F. Lach and Edwin J. Van Kley, *Asia in the Making of Europe*. Vol. III: *A Century of Advance, Book Four, East Asia* (Chicago: University of Chicago Press, 1994).

218 This was probably Artaxerxes I, fifth King of Kings of the Achaemenid Empire, from 465 to 424 B.C.E. He was the third son of Xerxes I and

grandson of Darius I. Our author here simply plays with learned knowledge of antiquity.

219 This was the ancient Assyrian city in Upper Mesopotamia, located on the outskirts of Mosul in modern-day northern Iraq. It is located on the eastern bank of the Tigris River and was the capital and largest city of the Neo-Assyrian Empire. Nineveh was first mentioned in the Bible, Genesis 10:11, and then it became the main setting of the Book of Tobit, and the Book of Jona, 3:3, and 4:11, refers to it as well. It is not uncommon for medieval writers who present 'factual' information to combine references to antiquity, classical mythology, and the Bible with their own observations or general knowledge.

220 Medieval authors assumed that four rivers flowed out of Paradise, again following the Old Testament, Genesis 2:10–14, where an unnamed stream flowing out of the Garden of Eden splits into four branches: Pishon, Gihon, Hiddekel (Tigris), and Phrath (Euphrates).

221 It originates in Turkey, then flows through modern-day Syria and Iraq, and joins the Tigris in the Shatt al-Arab, which empties into the Persian Gulf.

222 Halaam was probably meant to be Balaam, a well-known diviner mentioned in the Old Testament, or rather, Torah, chapters 22 and following in the Book of Numbers; hence we face here an odd merging of a historical figure with a biblical character.

223 A mythical reference, merging the story of the lost tribes of Israel with the apocalyptic peoples of Gog and Magog, commonly mentioned by writers of travelogues such as Marco Polo and John Mandeville.

224 Nebuchadnezzar II ruled from the time of the death of his father Nabopolassar in 605 B.C.E. to his own death in 562 B.C.E. He was regarded as the greatest ruler of the kingdom of Babylon and the longest-reigning king of the Chaldean dynasty. In 587 B.C.E., Nebuchadnezzar conquered and destroyed the kingdom of Judah, and its capital, Jerusalem. The destruction of Jerusalem led to the Babylonian captivity as the city's population, and people from the surrounding lands, were deported to Babylonia. For Jews, Nebuchadnezzar was one of their greatest enemies, and he was massively invested in building up his capital, which led to the notion of the Whore of Babylon. The Book of Jeremiah primarily retells the story of the Babylonian Captivity.

225 Those three cities are supposed to be Baghdad, Susa, and Beijing. Susa was c. 160 miles east of the river Tigris in modern-day Iran and was one of the major cities in antiquity. Modern-day Beijing had numerous name changes throughout time; Marco Polo called it Khanbaliq, or Cambuluc (see also below).

226 Obviously, the author relies heavily on Christians' concepts about their own religion to explain the structures of the Islamic religion, also in administrative terms.

Commentary

227 The anonymous author refers to older historical events involving the Armenians and Mongols. Hethum I (1213–1270) ruled the Armenian Kingdom of Cilicia (also known as 'Little Armenia') from 1226 to 1270.

228 The author indicates here that he had a considerable library available when he composed his treatise, which thus obviously consisted of his own memories and of written source material.

229 Susa was a major ancient city, first settled in c. 4200 B.C.E., in the lower Zagros Mountains about 160 miles east of the Tigris, between the Karkheh and Dez Rivers in modern-day Iran. Today, the Iranian city of Shush is located on the site of ancient Susa. It remains unclear why the author also refers to the name "Thauris," which is not confirmed in other sources. The biblical Book of Esther is set in the Persian capital of Susa (Shushan) in the third year of the reign of the Persian king Ahasuerus. The prophet Daniel from the Old Testament was said to have stayed in Susa, and the present mausoleum is venerated by Muslim pilgrims, but there are a handful of other cities that claim the same. The Mongols conquered Susa in 1218 – not in 1259, as Brall-Tuchel, p. 137, note 132, has it.

230 He refers here to the Persian king Ahasuerus (Ahasverus), who is the same as Xerxes. He ruled between 486 and 465 B.C.E. and is the one the Book of Esther deals with. After having removed his previous queen from her post because she had refused to dance in front of the palace guests wearing only her crown (naked?), Ahasuerus chose the orphan woman Esther as his new wife. She had been fostered by her first cousin Mordecai (maybe her uncle), who gains a post at the court and can expose two individuals who had tried to assassinate the king. Queen Esther later discovers yet another plot by the Viceroy Haman to have all Jews killed; and she skillfully turns this all around, which allows the Jews to kill Haman, his sons, and many of his people. Ahasuerus and Haman attend Esther's second banquet at which he promises to fulfil any of her wishes. Esther reveals her Jewish identity and begs for her own people and her own life. The ruler angrily leaves the room, and Haman falls upon Esther begging her to rescue him, but when her husband returns, he believes that Haman tried to rape her, which spells the end for him and his people, while the Jews then triumph and fare well, being able to kill thousands of their opponents. Until today, Jews celebrate this history during Purim.

231 This is an unusual formulation here: "Da is also vil aue geschreuen" (p. 351, 144r). Normally, the author only states that there would be much more to say about something, but here he also adds that other writers have already addressed the topic; so, he combines the oral and the written aspect, apparently because the legend of the barren tree had exerted such an influence. See the references in Brall-Tuchel, p. 139, note 134.

232 This date might help us further as a *terminus post quem*, that is, after which this account was written, but it does not require an assumption because the anonymous writer intended to date it around 1340.

Der Niederrheinische Orientbericht, c.1350

233 "Gratias," which should have been fully "Deo gratias," means, in Latin, 'Thanks,' or rather 'Thanks be to God,' and "Benedicite" means 'may it be blessed.' The first formula derived from the Vulgate text (Jerome's Bible) of 1 Corinthians 15:57 and 2 Corinthians 2:14. The second formula comes from Bible passages in the Book of Daniel (Dan. 3, 57–88 and 56) and Psalm 148. In its full version, it would be "Benedicite, omnia opera Domini!" (Blessed be all works of the Lord!). It usually follows the Holy Office of Lauds on Sundays and feast days.

234 The author shifts in the use of tenses here.

235 Although somewhat different in comparison with the common medieval narratives of the Amazons, the author here clearly refers to those mythical women living by themselves, being excellent masters of shooting with bow and arrows. There are, however, no comments about these women cutting off their right breast to improve their handling of their weapons. The Amazons are already mentioned in the ancient Greek accounts of Alexander the Great. See, for instance, Paul Lacour, *Les Amazones. Les femmes dans l'histoire* (Paris: Perrin, 1901); Josine H. Blok, *The Early Amazons: Modern and Ancient Perspectives on a Persistent Myth*. Religions in the Graeco-Roman World, 120 (Leiden and Boston: Brill, 1996); Patrick J. Geary, *Women at the Beginning: Origin Myths from the Amazons to the Virgin Mary* (Princeton, NJ: Princeton University Press, 2006); Adrienne Mayor, *The Amazons: Lives and Legends of Warrior Women Across the Ancient World* (Princeton, NJ: Princeton University Press, 2014).

236 This is a marvelous example of the complete reversal of gender roles. There is virtually only one other case of such a situation, equally playfully projected, that is, in the anonymous *chantefable* "Aucassin et Nicolette," c. 1240 (or earlier). Here, the two protagonists encounter such a reversal in the kingdom of Torelore, where the queen fights on the battlefield (though only with foodstuffs) and where the king lies in bed, assuming that he is with child. See the English translation, along with the Old French original, by Katharine Margot Toohey, online at https://quemarpress.weebly.com/uploads/8/6/1/4/86149566/aucassin_and_nicolette_-_translation_by_k.m._toohey.pdf (last accessed on Oct. 8, 2022). The translations are good, but the illustrations are just ridiculous.

237 It is not clear why the author uses both terms for the Asian continent, "van oisten vnd van orienten" (p. 357, 145v).

238 Indeed, throughout medieval Europe, Catholic churches show images of Saint Christopher both on the outside and the inside (frescoes, sculptures, and paintings). He was said to have been a giant (Canaanite) who searched for a lord whom he could serve. Each time, however, when he believed he had found one, it turned out that this lord was still subservient to another one (king, devil, Christ). Frustrated, Christopher settled at a river and from then on carried people across the water. One day, a small child knocked on his door to be transported. The giant happily did so, but

Commentary

in the middle of the river, the weight of the child grew tremendously, and the giant was afraid of drowning. Upon being asked who he really is, the child reveals that he is Christ, and that hence Christopher is carrying the entire world and its lord. The best-known version of this religious legend can be found in the *Legenda aurea* by Jacobus de Voragine (thirteenth century). Originally, Christopher was said to have been a martyr killed in the fourth or early fifth century C.E. Despite the long tradition of Christopher's alleged sainthood, it was dropped in 1970 as part of the general reorganization of the calendar of the Roman rite. Nevertheless, Christopher is still worshipped as a saint for travelers, mariners, ferrymen, and athletes, and he is regarded as one of the Fourteen Holy Helpers ("Nothelfer"), a notion that emerged in the Rhineland during the fourteenth century, probably in response to the Black Death. People prayed and appealed to those helpers, such as Saint Barbara, Saint Margaret, and Saint Catherine, in many different emergencies.

239 Here we have firm evidence that the author had learned some basic features of Buddhism, i.e., the concept of rebirth until the individual is permitted to enter Nirvana. It is true that he presents only fragmentary aspects and does not understand any of the religious subtleties, but this passage still deserves close attention as evidence of intellectual/religious exchanges between East and West. See Albrecht Classen, "Kulturelle und religiöse Kontakte zwischen dem christlichen Europa und dem buddhistischen Indien während des Mittelalters: Rudolfs von Ems *Barlaam und Josaphat* im europäischen Kontext," *Fabula* 41.3/4 (2000): 203–28; id., "Global Middle Ages: Eastern Wisdom (Buddhistic) Teachings in Medieval European Literature. With a Focus on *Barlaam and Josaphat*," *Humanities and Social Science Research* 4.2 (2021): 10–20; https://doi.org/10.30560/hssr.v4n2p10; or: https://j.ideasspread.org/index.php/hssr/article/view/916; id., "Early Encounters with Buddhism: Some Medieval European Travelogue Authors Offer First Insights into a Foreign Religion. Explorations of an Unchartered Territory," to appear in *The East Asian Journal of Philosophy*, special issue, *Dynamic Encounters between Buddhism and the West*, ed. Laura Langone. See also Romedio Schmitz-Esser, "The Buddha and the Medieval West: Changing Perspectives on Cultural Exchange between Asia and Europe in the Middle Ages," *Travel, Time, and Space in the Middle Ages and Early Modern Time: Explorations of World Perceptions and Processes of Identity Formation*, ed. Albrecht Classen. Fundamentals of Medieval and Early Modern Culture, 22 (Berlin and Boston: Walter de Gruyter, 2018), 311–30.

240 The reference here is unclear, and the syntax does not make good sense. The author generally means that those odd peoples populate the various courts and are welcome as exotic or curious creatures.

241 This might well be the most important sentence in the entire treatise insofar as the author acknowledges the foundation of tolerance, paying

Der Niederrheinische Orientbericht, *c.1350*

full respect to the foreign peoples and undermining any Eurocentric perspective because there is no reason for him to regard himself and his world in any sense superior to the East. I have put the sentence in bold to highlight its importance. The original is: "de dunkent, dat wir also seltzen sin, als sy vns dunckent" (p. 359, 146v).

242 This does not mean that the merchants were not Christians. Instead, the author wants to discriminate again between clerics and secular travelers.

243 He reflects here on the method of haggling, negotiations, and bartering common in the eastern world.

244 This is a typical example of the author's somewhat clumsy style, but he wants to be precise as to the occasions when it rains, so he has to repeat the phrase.

245 Michaelmas is the Feast of Michael, Gabriel, and Raphael, that is, the Feast of the Archangels, or the Feast of Saint Michael and All Angels, which is celebrated on Sept. 29. Michaelmas was one of the four quarter days of the English and Irish financial, judicial, and academic year, so the fall semester began on Michaelmas, a practice that is no longer generally observed. Michaelmas is a contraction of Michael's Mass, like Christmas, Christ's Mass.

246 Meaning, when an earthquake takes place and people are afraid of death.

247 It is typical for all reports of that kind to be presented in comparative terms for the western readers to better understand the different world. This also implies that the author definitely recognized cultural parallels.

248 This is about 9 inches; cf. this online dictionary (in German): https://blog.histofakt.de/?p=3399#:~:text=Meist%20entsprach%20er%20der%20Fl%C3%A4che,bis%20zu%2012.000%20Quadratmeter%20gebr%C3%A4uchlich.&text=Das%20M%C3%BCnzpfund%20war%2016%20Unzen%20schwer. For good images to explain this, see https://de.wikipedia.org/wiki/Spanne_(L%C3%A4ngenma%C3%9F) (last accessed on Oct. 9). Cf. also the contributions to *Sourcebook in the Mathematics of Medieval Europe and North Africa*, ed. Victor J. Katz, Menso Folkerts, Barnabas Hughes, Roi Wagner, and J. Lennart Berggren (Princeton, NJ, and Oxford: Princeton University Press, 2016) (however, this is more on mathematics than on measures in practical terms!).

249 Shrovetide is 49 days before Easter, so the date shifts every year.

250 This might refer to orange trees for which this phenomenon is quite common.

251 He means that if they have to work or travel, they would do that only at night.

252 Brall-Tuchel's translation into modern German is confusing or even misleading since he implies that the burning of incense and cinnamon is done in order to fill the streets with smoke. The text only says that the consequence of the burning is that the streets are filled with smoke: "dat alle straissen vol rochs sint" (p. 152; Micklin, p. 365, fol. 148r).

Commentary

253 The *elle* is the distance between the elbow and the tip of the middle finger, so c. 50–80 cm, i.e., a cubit. The *elle*, normally used to measure cloth, consists of the equivalent of six palms or two spans.

254 It is not clear what the author means here since the term he uses implies moral criticism; "unstede" only says, in simple terms, 'unsteady,' which could mean various things, such as moving around a lot, or even disloyalty, readiness to commit adultery, though I doubt that the author might have had that also in mind. But since the women in the Arabic world are thus described as not bound to the house, maybe moving around the city regularly, visiting friends and relatives, the anonymous author might have harbored moral concerns.

255 Acre was the last Christian fortress, and once it had fallen to the Mamluks in 1291 under the leadership of Al-Ashraf Salāh ad-Dīn Khalil ibn Qalawūn, the eighth Bahri Mamluk Sultan, who was assassinated in 1293, the end of the crusading history had been reached.

256 Muslims are not allowed to drink alcohol according to the Qur'an, 5:90: "O believers! Intoxicants, gambling, idols, and drawing lots for decisions are all evil of Satan's handiwork. So shun them so you may be successful."

257 It seems illogical that the author suddenly refers to India. The description of the building strategy is obviously missing some crucial elements since there is no word about the mortar, if any was used.

258 In other words, French was the *lingua franca* among the elite, whereas the rural population spoke Arabic, or another local language.

259 Brall-Tuchel, p. 159, reads the preposition "achter" only as 'after,' or 'behind,' but it could also mean 'across' or 'around'; see Gerhard Köbler, *Mittelniederdeutsches Wörterbuch*, 3rd ed., 2014, online at: https://www.koeblergerhard.de/mnd/mnd_a.html (last accessed on Oct. 9, 2022).

260 The author uses the spelling of "Basant," which Brall-Tuchel replicates, but the proper spelling is "bezant" (Old French 'besant,' from Latin 'bizantius aureus'). It was a term mostly used in the west for a Byzantine coin out of gold. Later, as in our case, 'besant' designated the gold dinars produced by Islamic governments. See the useful website: https://en.wikipedia.org/wiki/Bezant (last accessed on Oct. 9, 2022).

261 It is extremely difficult to determine the exact value of medieval currency. Here, however, the poet relates the knight's income with the actual cost of maintaining two horses, including all the equipment, food, servants, stable, etc. It is not clear why the servants' incomes would vary so much. Maybe the reason was the knight's personal condition and wealth.

262 This is not quite clear from the text: "spyse und voder" (158; Micklin, p. 371, 149v: "spijse vnd voder"), but if we keep in mind the great need of fodder for the horses [hay], which was certainly expensive, then our translation would make sense.

263 This is a kind of lance game, normally preparing the participants for a joust. Everyone, whether a knight or not, could participate in it. The quintain

Der Niederrheinische Orientbericht, *c.1350*

itself was normally a wooden plate or a mannequin at which the lances were launched to practice for a real joust. See Juliet R. V. Barker, *The Tournament in England: 1100–1400* (Woodbridge: Boydell Press, 1986); Lucien Clare, *Quintaine, la course de bague et le jeu de têtes* (Paris: Ed. du CNRS, 1983). For good explanations and some helpful images, see https://en.wikipedia.org/wiki/Quintain_(jousting) (last accessed on Oct. 10, 2022).

264 He argues, in other words, that the Muslim knights who are familiar with their Christian counterparts have become acculturated and follow the lifestyle of their European colleagues.

265 This sounds almost democratic since only the social group is said to have any say with regard to the power distribution.

266 Literally, neither pleading nor money can prevent that, only the knight's life.

267 He refers to a "schrift" (p. 160; 'writing'; Micklin, p. 373, 150r) but does not specify this further. At any rate, he identifies one of his sources in general terms . Maybe he had the Bible in mind?

268 As simplistic as this sentence might be, the author indicates a. that public life in Cairo or elsewhere was characterized by a multiplicity of different cultures, all existing peacefully next to each other, and b. that he himself could not fathom all of them sufficiently. This open admission underscores particularly the multicultural conditions in the world of the eastern Mediterranean.

269 Theriac was, since antiquity, an odd concoction of many different substances, allegedly a panacea against all kinds of sicknesses, the plague, snake bites, etc. Its long preparation process made it very expensive; whether it was effective cannot be determined today; for a good introduction, see https://en.wikipedia.org/wiki/Theriac (last accessed on Oct. 10, 2022). Gilbert Watson, *Theriac and Mithridatium: A Study in Therapeutics.* Publications of the Welcome Historical Medical Library, N.S., 9 (London: The Welcome Histor. Med. Library, 1966). See now also Danuta Raj, Katarzyna Pękacka-Falkowska, Maciej Włodarczyk, and Jakub Węglorz, "The Real Theriac – Panacea, Poisonous Drug or Quackery?," *J Ethnopharmacol* 281 (2021 Dec 5:114535. doi: 10.1016/j.jep.2021.114535. Epub 2021 Aug. 17).

270 This is a typical formula, combining the oral with the written account, because the report was read out aloud and hence listened to by those who could not read. In the fourteenth century, the literacy rate was still very low, even in urban centers such as Cologne. See Manfred Günter Scholz, *Hören und Lesen: Studien zur primären Rezeption der Literatur im 12. und 13. Jahrhundert* (Wiesbaden: Steiner, 1980); for the late Middle Ages and early modern time, see Ingeborg Spriewald, *Literatur zwischen Hören und Lesen: Wandel von Funktion und Rezeption im späten Mittelalter. Fallstudien zu Beheim, Folz und Sachs* (Berlin: Aufbau-Verlag, 1990). See now the contributions to *Orality and Literacy in the Middle Ages: Essays on*

Commentary

a Conjunction and its Consequences in Honour of D. H. Green, ed. Mark Chinca and Christopher Young. Utrecht Studies in Medieval Literacy, 12 (Turnhout: Brepols, 2005).

271 Brall-Tuchel, p. 165, note 143, suspects that it might be a kind of antelope, but cannot be more specific either.

272 The list begins with plurals, and ends with singulars, so I have changed everything to plural.

273 The author might also mean that people have observed the lion's true character, or nature.

274 Here we encounter another example of the author referring to his written sources, although he is not specific about the respective titles.

275 This means that the leopard protects its lord very diligently.

276 Up to this point, he might have meant a rhinoceros; the following, however, moves into the realm of myth once again.

277 This is an addition from ms. A. We find an almost identical description of the colorful fur of the famous dog Petitcreiu in Gottfried von Strassburg's *Tristan and Isolde* (c. 1210). Gottfried von Strassburg, *Tristan and Isolde* with Ulrich von Türheim's *Continuation*, ed. and trans., with an intro., by William T. Whobrey (Indianapolis, IN, and Cambridge: Hackett Publishing, 2020), ch. 23, 195–201.

278 Literally: very funny animal.

279 The author suddenly switches from the plural to the singular.

280 Brall-Tuchel, p. 167, uses the noun 'repentance,' which does not make sense here.

281 There are too many conceptual errors here to describe them in detail. We are, after all, still in the fourteenth century, and the author was certainly not a carefully observing biologist. Instead, both here and throughout, he combined learned knowledge with his own observations, which explains the repeated syntactical errors or convoluted, repetitive structure.

282 The switch from singular to plural is in the original. Some of the comments about the other animals are very fanciful.

283 This side comment is only found in a marginal note and does not make much sense, unless the commentator thought that the buffalo was already domesticated.

284 Here is a great example showing the proximity of Middle Low German and Middle English: "groff" (p. 170; Micklin p. 383, 152v) means, 'gruff,' although the author probably means something more like 'sturdy' or 'mighty.'

285 He does not really mean teeth, but the elephant's tusks.

286 An *âme* or *ôme* is the measure of a vessel which a donkey or a horse can carry on its back, filled with water, so c. 130 to 150 kg, or c. 134 to 150 liters.

287 He certainly meant to say, 'back,' but the text clearly has "hals" (172, 'neck') because it is considered the extension of the head in a horizontal position.

Der Niederrheinische Orientbericht, *c.1350*

288 Here we learn that the author draws on his own experience; at least, he insists that he knows more about elephants than most people in the West.

289 The entire account of the dragon seems to be pure fantasy. The dragon appears countless times in many different cultures throughout time, both in the Middle Ages and in the modern world, both in the East and in the West.

290 Meaning: has drowned, is rotted and is hence ready to be eaten by the crocodile. Crocodiles are stalk-and-ambush predators, and they consume a wide variety of prey, often only after the carcass has started to rot.

291 The *Vitae Patrum* (The Lives of the Fathers), or the *Lives of the Desert Fathers*, were hagiographical texts about the desert saints in Egypt and the Near East (men and women, anchorites, hermits, monks), written originally in Greek, and first translated into Latin between the fourth and seventh centuries. The Dominican friar Domenico Cavalca from Pisa created the first vernacular translation (into Italian) in the early fourteenth century. The most famous text in this loosely compiled corpus was the life of Saint Anthony. A famous female example was the life of Maria Aegyptiaca. Our author, who was certainly not theologically educated, had only a general knowledge of this collection.

292 Here is a good example to illustrate the vast range of meanings which individual High or Low Middle German words could have: "vrume" can mean 'worthy,' 'virtuous,' 'honorable,' 'valid,' 'strong,' 'powerful,' 'dignified,' or 'useful.'

293 The florin was a gold coin struck in Florence, Italy, between c. 1252 and 1533, with no noticeable change in its gold content. It enjoyed the status of representing a global standard in currency during the late Middle Ages.

294 Brall-Tuchel, p. 179, contracts this sentence too much; I render the full sentence, adding the note on cleanliness.

295 This is a kind of bread used to dip into sauces or to wipe off fat. Here I follow Brall-Tuchel's explanation, p. 179, n. 146.

296 Neither the syntax nor the content are very clear; the author seems to confuse things or expresses himself rather confusingly.

297 Here, the original is repetitive, illogical, and unclear.

298 It seems as if the author is simply utilizing fiction here without thinking clearly what he might be saying.

299 All this follows more or less the late antique *Physiologus* (c. second century C.E.), first translated from Greek into Latin around 400, and represents a half-digested version of the ancient Greek text with its allegorical meaning – allegorical exegesis.

300 Brall-Tuchel, p. 185, translates "rouff" ('call') as 'luring song,' which might go beyond what the author had in mind.

301 Certainly an exaggeration and an indication that the author writes a lot from hearsay in this case.

Commentary

302 The poet obviously admits that the story of the phoenix amounts to a myth, as much as he tries to confirm its existence through the following sentence. The myth of this bird that self-immolates and then rises from its ashes once again served as a powerful and timeless symbol of rebirth. Major writers from antiquity through the Middle Ages such as Herodotus, Lucan, Pliny the Elder, Ovid, Pope Clement I, Lactantius, and Isidore of Seville contributed to the development of the myth. The phoenix is depicted in countless art works and literary texts. The earliest reference might well be in a fragment of the Precepts of Chiron, attributed to the ancient Greek poet Hesiod (sixth century B.C.E.). According to Herodotus (fifth century B.C.E.), the phoenix originated in Egypt: "The Egyptians] have also another sacred bird called the phoenix which I myself have never seen, except in pictures. Indeed, it is a great rarity, even in Egypt, only coming there (according to the accounts of the people of Heliopolis) once in five hundred years, when the old phoenix dies. Its size and appearance, if it is like the pictures, are as follow: The plumage is partly red, partly golden, while the general appearance and size are almost exactly that of the eagle. They tell a story of what this bird does, which does not seem to me to be credible: that he comes all the way from Arabia, and brings the parent bird, all plastered over with myrrh, to the temple of the Sun, and there buries the body." Here quoted from https://en.wikipedia.org/wiki/Phoenix_(mythology)#cite_ref-RAWLINSON-1848_9-0 (last accessed on Oct. 13, 2022). Cf. the critical edition and translation, Herodot, *Historien*. Two vols. *Griechisch–deutsch*, ed. Josef Feix. 7th ed. Sammlung Tusculum (Berlin: Akademie-Verlag, 2011), 2, 73. See *The Phoenix*, ed. N. F. Blake. Old and Middle English Texts (Manchester: Manchester University Press, 1964); R. van den Broek, *The Myth of the Phoenix – According to Classical and Early Christian Traditions*. Etudes préliminaires aux religions orientales dans l'empire romain, 24 (Leiden: Brill, 1972); Thomas Honegger, *From Phoenix to Chauntecleer: Medieval English Animal Poetry*. Schweizer anglistische Arbeiten, 120 (Tübingen: Francke, 1996).

303 This is a rather common inexpressibility topos which the author resorts to whenever he wants to underscore the exceptionality and extreme beauty of something, like the Sultan's treasure or natural beauty.

304 Although the anonymous writer primarily discusses the world of Arabia, he rarely uses this term, which hence carries considerable weight in the current context since the phoenix was at any rate a mythical bird. Its association with Arabia serves here to intensify the fabulous nature of the world of the Near East.

305 Another spelling in medieval Latin was "charadrius," or "caladris," which was close to "calandris" or 'lark,' the only bird that sings while hovering in the air. In the Vulgate (Jerome), the Hebrew term "anaphah" (unclean bird) was translated as "charadrios," which Luther in turn equated with the "Calidris," which biologists today identify with a migratory but wading

bird originating in the Arctic, belonging to the family of Scolopacidae. He understood this to be a heron, so he translated it as "Reiher." Since the author drew from mythological information, we do not need to attempt to identify it as an existing bird.

306 According to mythology, this bird is the caladrius, allegedly a purely white bird with no spot of another color on its plumage or body. It has been associated with the dove, the heron, or the plover. In medieval bestiaries, the caladrius is said to perform the same function as described by our anonymous author, except that there it only needs to look into the eyes of the sick person, then flies high up and releases the sickness there where the sun destroys it, which also protects the bird. The identification of the caladrius or caradrius, as it is spelled here, with Christ, is self-explanatory. See, for instance, George C. Druce, "The Caladrius and Its Legend, Sculptured Upon the Twelfth-Century Doorway of Alne Church, Yorkshire," *Archaeological Journal* 69 (1912): 381–416. The caladrius is, of course, included in the *Physiologus* as one of the major mythological beasts. For the relevant scholarship and also a good overview of the mythical history, see https://de.wikipedia.org/wiki/Caladrius (last accessed on Oct. 13, 2022).

307 This statement is, to say the least, astonishing, if not simply an expression of utter ignorance, since storks regularly migrate from northern Europe (Netherlands, Germany, Poland, etc.) to Egypt and other North African lands, crossing either the Strait of Gibraltar (western route) or Turkey, i.e., the Bosporus, then via Israel and the Sinai (eastern route), from where they tend to continue to southern Egypt and Sudan, and further on to eastern Africa. For the latest research on storks and their migratory behavior today, also with a good map, photos, and much cultural–historical background, see https://de.wikipedia.org/wiki/Wei%C3%9Fstorch#Zugverhalten (last accessed on Oct. 13, 2022). Cf. now esp. John H. Rappole, *The Avian Migrant: The Biology of Bird Migration* (New York: Columbia University Press, 2013); Mike Unwin and David Tipling, *Flights of Passage: An Illustrated Natural History of Bird Migration* (New Haven, CT, and London: Yale University Press, 2020).

308 This is also a rather problematic statement because swallows migrate from Africa or South America north to Europe and North America in early spring, and in the opposite direction in late summer/early fall. However, perhaps the anonymous author refers here to the migration of swallows from South Africa to Egypt, which would be parallel to the migration of the European swallows. For a more popular but useful website, see https://www.discoverwildlife.com/animal-facts/birds/facts-about-swallows/; for the migration patterns of American swallows, see https://journeynorth.org/tm/swallow/News.html; or https://www.brinvale.com/swallow-migration-facts.htm (all last accessed on Oct. 13, 2022). Cf. esp. *Collins Atlas of Bird Migration: Tracing the Great Journeys of the World's Birds*, ed. Jonathan Elphick (London: Harper Collins, 1995).

Commentary

309 Brall-Tuchel, p. 187, n. 147, rightly suspects that the author means "Eisvogel" or Alcedinida; in English 'kingfisher.

310 What the author mentions about the conflict between eagles and falcons, and this in Egypt, is, to say the least, somewhat odd. There is no good explanation for this comment.

311 This means, of course, that the falcon, or whatever bird of prey, sits on a glove; otherwise, the claw would quickly and easily penetrate the hunter's skin and hurt him badly.

312 He might mean the personal competition among different falconers.

313 The author uses the word "patryse," which Brall-Tuchel (p. 189) does not know how to translate. The *Oxford English Dictionary* offers this etymology: "Anglo-Norman and Old French perdriz, pertriz (c1170; Middle French, French perdrix; in Anglo-Norman also pardis, pardriz, partriz, partreiz), alteration of Anglo-Norman perdix (c1119 < classical Latin perdīc-, perdīx partridge < ancient Greek πέρδικ-, πέρδιξ partridge (usually the rock partridge or the chukar partridge), probably < πέρδεσθαι to break wind (see fart v.; perhaps after the noise made by the bird as it flies away" (https://www-oed-com.ezproxy1.library.arizona.edu/view/Entry/138325?rskey=yIJBCw&result=1&isAdvanced=false#eid). The anonymous author must have heard the French word while he lived in the Middle East and rendered it into his Middle Low German without changing it. The word "patryse," however, does not appear in the relevant Middle High and Middle Low German dictionaries, so it might well be a *hapax legomenon* within the German language area.

314 Those partridges and chickens probably disturbed the hunt and the falconers wanted to chase them away.

315 Perhaps a form of acacia. It might be a *Rhododendron niveum*, also known as a sikkim tree, a rhododendron species native to northeastern India (including Sikkim), Bhutan, and southern Tibet in China, and apparently also present in the Near East, such as Egypt. See also, for example, for many good illustrations, https://treesandshrubsonline.org/articles/rhododendron/rhododendron-niveum/

316 He means, specifically, the fig-mulberry (Lat.: Ficus sycomorus), which carries that name because the figs resemble the mulberry.

317 That is exactly the same word as is still used in modern German.

318 The author probably had the *Rhododendron niveum in mind*, native to northeastern India (including Sikkim), Bhutan, and southern Tibet in China. It grows either as a shrub or can reach the height of a tree.

319 He does not mean specifically 'cold' in terms of temperature; instead, with 'cold' he refers to one of the four humors allegedly determining all of human life according to the ancient medical doctor Galen. Each one of those humors represented a type of character.

320 It would seem too far-fetched to associate this tree with the Brazil tree (*Paubrasilia*) since that was only discovered by Portuguese explorers in

South America in the early sixteenth century. But it is a relative of an Asian species of sappanwood or Indian redwood used already in the Middle Ages after its importation from India. Brall-Tuchel, p. 191, suspects that this "Brunsilien Houlz" might be a type of "Johannisbrotbaum," or "Ceratonia siliqua," which is quite common in the eastern Mediterranean and the Middle East. This would be the carob shrub or tree: "a flowering evergreen tree or shrub in the Caesalpinioideae sub-family of the legume family, Fabaceae. It is widely cultivated for its edible pods, and as an ornamental tree in gardens and landscapes. The carob tree is native to the Mediterranean region and the Middle East" (quoted from https://en.wikipedia.org/wiki/Carob; last accessed on Oct. 13, 2022).

321 This would be the Tree Aloe, or *Aloidendron barberae*, which is the largest species of aloe growing in Africa; see https://www.gardenia.net/plant/aloidendron-barberae (last accessed on March 8, 2023). See Ernst J. Van Jaarsveld and Eric Judd, *Tree Aloes of Africa* (Cape Town: Penrock Publications, 2015). Konrad von Megenberg, in his *'Das Buch der Natur': Untersuchungen zu seiner Text- und Überlieferungsgeschichte.* Münchener Texte und Untersuchungen zur deutschen Literatur des Mittelalters, 110 (Tübingen: Max Niemeyer, 1998), first written around 1360 and first printed in 1475, uses almost the same phrases to describe this wood: (in my translation) "Aloe is a wood and a tree that grows in India and in Arabia, as Isidore says [Isidore of Seville], and it has a good sweet smell. The other masters say that this wood comes from the earthly paradise floating on water; and people catch it with nets from the water" (386). If our anonymous author drew that information from Konrad, we would have to date his text really late, perhaps around 1360. However, the existence of many other similar 'scientific' texts at that time make this claim rather tenuous.

322 Again, an 'elle' is a measuring unit, c. 50 to 60 cm long.

323 He probably had in mind persimmons, although the specific description given then does not quite fit what we know today about this tree. Nevertheless, the similarities are striking enough to support the claim that the "paradise apple" is a persimmon. See https://en.wikipedia.org/wiki/Persimmon (last accessed on Oct. 13, 2022).

324 This would be, in its Latin term, *Maclura pomifera*, commonly known as the Osage orange, or horse apple, but which is native only to the south-central United States. The author had some other types of apples in mind, if not an entirely different fruit looking like an apple.

325 He probably means with 'cooling' rather 'quenching one's thirst.'

326 This is the "*Ficus sycomorus*," called the 'sycamore fig' or the 'fig-mulberry' because of the similarities in appearance with those fruit.

327 He probably meant that the asparagus becomes too fibrous if it grows old, which makes it unpalatable.

328 The author only says "Zucker" (sugar), but since he addresses the growth of a plant, it can only be sugar cane.

Commentary

329 This is Latin for sugar cane, literally 'honey ear.' The word is closely related with 'caramel,' borrowed from the French 'caramel,' from the Spanish 'caramelo,' from Late Latin 'calamellus,' diminutive of 'calamus' ("reed"), or alternatively from Medieval Latin 'cannamellis,' which is either a compound of 'canna' + 'mellis' or possibly a borrowing from Arabic. See https://en.wiktionary.org/wiki/karamel; and OED at https://www-oed-com.ezproxy2.library.arizona.edu/view/Entry/27703?rskey=InUqgt&result=1#eid (both last accessed on Oct. 13, 2022).

330 This is an attempt to make sense of the original which only says that 'there is much uncultivated land between them,' though it cannot mean that the individual stalks grow far apart from each other. It is a common practice even now to interrupt the regular cycle of growing crops in the fields to allow them to rest and regenerate, thus regaining their natural fertilizers and interrupting if not killing any potential soil pathogens.

331 He uses the word "beirwirtz," which Brall-Tuchel, p. 195, translates literally as 'beer spice.' This is the liquid that oozes out of the brewing water. According to an online source, "Würze ist die Flüssigkeit, welche während des Läuterns aus dem Brauwasser, dem Hopfen und dem gelösten Malzzucker entsteht" (https://brauen.de/braulexikon/wuerze/; last accessed on Oct. 14, 2022; The spice is the liquid which is created during the lautering of the brewing water, the hop, and the dissolved malt sugar). 'Lautering' is the beer brewing process during which the mash is separated into clear liquid wort and residual grain.

332 This is September 17. See https://www.heiligenlexikon.de/BiographienL/Lambert_von_Maastricht.html (last accessed on Oct. 14, 2022).

333 He cuts short the logical sequence to connect with the beginning of his account, leaving out the various steps described above.

334 He means, of course, in shorthand, sugar cane and only then the sugar itself as it is produced from the cane.

335 See the explanation of this coin above, note 260.

336 See the explanation of this Florentine coin above, note 293.

337 The word used here is "Purpone," which does not exist in any dictionary, not even in the Middle Low German dictionary by Karl Schiller and August Lübben, *Mittelniederdeutsches Wörterbuch*. Fotomechanischer Neudruck der Ausgabe 1875– (Vaduz, Liechtenstein: Sändig-Repr.-Verlag Wohlwend, 1968–). Online at: https://www.koeblergerhard.de/Fontes/Luebben_MittelniederdeutschesHandwoerterbuch1888.pdf. See also https://www.niederdeutsche-literatur.de/autoren/index.php; (both last accessed on Oct. 22, 2022). Brall-Tuchel, p. 197, translates this as "pumpkin," which cannot be right at all because that fruit originated from the New World and cannot be eaten at any rate without having been cooked and well prepared. The better option seems to be the "Pampelmuse," or 'pomelo,' though that word entered the German language from the Dutch only in the eighteenth century (known in Dutch as "pompelmoes" or "pampelmoes"

129

only since 1648). Etymologically, 'pampel' in Dutch means 'large,' whereas 'limoese' derives from Portuguese, meaning 'citrus.' And, to problematize the issue further, the modern grapefruit resulted only from the genetic crossing of the pomelo with the orange. Our best bet seems to be that "purpone" represents some kind of a citrus fruit common in the Near East, perhaps simply the orange or a variant species. 'Purpone' seems to be a *hapax legomenon* in Middle Low and Middle High German. However, in late medieval cookery or recipe books, we find references to the *Citrus × aurantium* or 'bitter orange' (also 'Seville orange'). The German word commonly used was 'Pomeranze,' derived from Latin 'pomum aurantium' ('golden apple') since the fifteenth century; cf. the *Deutsches Wörterbuch* by the Brothers Grimm, https://woerterbuchnetz.de/?sigle=DWB&lem-id=P06298#0. For practical information on this fruit, see https://de.wiki-pedia.org/wiki/Bitterorange. For its use in late medieval cooking recipes, see Elvira Glaser, "Schweizer Kochbuchhandschriften im spätmittelalter-lichen-frühneuzeitlichen Kulturkontakt," *Cibo e salute nelle tradizioni germaniche medievali / Food and Health in the Germanic Middle Ages*, ed. Chiara Benati and Claudia Händl. *Filologia Germanica / Germanic Philology*, Supplemento 3 (Milan: Prometheus, 2022), 119–39; here 123. I thank the editors for sharing a PDF of this book which I later received as a hard copy (see my review in *sehepunkte* 22.11 (2022), online at: http://www.sehepunkte.de/2022/11/37376.html). Since the sourness of this fruit, i.e., its high degree of acidity, creates a strong reaction in the body when it is consumed, it makes good sense that the author says that it has to be eaten with honey to compensate for the bitter or sour taste (hence its property of being or causing cold). This fruit was imported to Andalusia by the Arabs as early as the tenth century and spread from there, reaching Italy in the eleventh century. It was commonly planted in the eastern Mediterranean, hence also in Egypt and Syria, so it makes good sense that our author was familiar with it. For biological, medical, and culinary background, see https://de.wikipedia.org/wiki/Bitterorange and https://www.nccih.nih.gov/health/bitter-orange (all last accessed on Oct. 23, 2022).

338 Again, this is a reference to the four humors, with a pomelo, a grapefruit, or rather the bitter orange allegedly contributing to the rise of the cold humor too much, which would endanger the body's balance of humors, and hence lead to sickness. If this is the pomelo, grapefruit, or Seville orange (see above), the author might have rightly thought of its high level of acidity, which would have indeed impacted the humoral balance negatively.

339 According to the Old Testament, Joshua was one of the twelve spies of Israel sent by Moses to explore the land of Canaan. In Numbers 13:1, after the death of Moses he was said to have led the Israelite tribes in the conquest of Canaan, where he allocated lands to the tribes. In Numbers 24:29, we are told: "After these things Joshua the son of Nun, the servant

Commentary

of the LORD, died, being 110 years old. And they buried him in his own inheritance at Timnath-serah, which is in the hill country of Ephraim, north of the mountain of Gaash." Quoted from https://www.esv.org/Joshua+24/ (last accessed on Oct. 14, 2022). The author identifies the Holy Land as the location where the bitter oranges commonly grow.

340 Manna was an edible substance like bread which God provided for the Israelites during their travels in the desert in the forty-year period after the Exodus and prior to the conquest of Canaan. See Exodus 16:1–36 and Numbers 11:1–9. Since biblical times, food was a crucial object in miracle accounts, and our author also reminds us of that in this and other passages. See Patrizia Lendinara, "Food Miracles in the Early Lives of St Cuthbert," *Cibo e salute nelle tradizioni germaniche medievali / Food and Health in the Germanic Middle Ages*, ed. Chiara Benati and Claudia Händl. *Filologia Germanica / Germanic Philology*, Supplemento 3 (Milan: Prometheus, 2022), 189–223; here 191–92.

341 In Middle High German, the word is generally spelled only as "ingewër," or "ingeber." In Middle Low German, it is spelled as "ingever," "inghever," "ingeber," or "incheber," and in other versions as "ingever" and "ingever," in Latin as "ingiber," or gingiber." The *Oxford English Dictionary*, which certainly comes to our assistance here because of the proximity between Middle English and Middle Low German, lists these variants: "Old English gingifer, Old English gingifr- (inflected form), early Middle English gingiferan (accusative), early Middle English gingeuir, early Middle English gingiber, early Middle English gingiuere, early Middle English gingiure, early Middle English gingyfran (accusative), early Middle English giniure, early Middle English gyngyfere (accusative), Middle English gingefere, Middle English gingiuer, Middle English gingyuer, Middle English guingyur, Middle English gyngeffre, Middle English gyngener (transmission error), Middle English gyngeuere, Middle English gyngever, Middle English gyngevre, Middle English gyngiuer, Middle English gyngynyr (transmission error), Middle English gyngyuer, Middle English gyngyure, Middle English zinziber, 1500s ȝenȝybyr; N.E.D. (1899) also records a form of late Middle English zenzyber." The anonymous writer uses the terms "Galegain Cedewar ind Genver" (196), referring to two different types of ginger.

342 It is highly possible that the author had something else in mind than 'thyme,' although he uses the word "Tymeanien," which Brall-Tuchel (p. 199) translates as 'thyme.' The following description does not make real sense concerning the harvesting of thyme, which is an aromatic perennial evergreen herb.

343 Those are sour cherries (*Prunus cerasus*), which tend to grow primarily in Bavaria, Austria, and Switzerland. Their consumption has demonstrated positive effects on a variety of physical ailments and infections. For a

detailed discussion, see https://de.wikipedia.org/wiki/Sauerkirsche (last accessed on Sept. 19, 2023).

344 In Latin, "*Cytisus scoparius*," which is native to western and central Europe. In German, it is "Ginster" and "Brambusch," which explains the use of the term "Braim" in our text.

345 Brall-Tuchel (p. 199) overemphasizes the term "wert" as "expensive." In the following section, the author himself uses the specific term "dure" for 'expensive in commercial terms.

346 The text is somewhat unclear; literally, it says: the lords and ladies burn water from them. Brall-Tuchel (p. 199) translates this exactly that way, but it really seems to refer to the production of perfume, maybe by means of drying those leaves.

347 The author is mistaken here, believing that the color scarlet derives from red berries. As we learn online, however, "Dactylopius is a genus of insect in the superfamily Coccoidea, the scale insects. It is the only genus in the family Dactylopiidae. These insects are known commonly as cochineals, a name that also specifically refers to the best-known species, the cochineal (Dactylopius coccus). The cochineal is an insect of economic and historical importance as a main source of the red dye carmine." Quoted from: https://en.wikipedia.org/wiki/Dactylopius. As to the production of the color scarlet, or carmine, see https://en.wikipedia.org/wiki/Carmine#Production (both last accessed on Oct. 14, 2022).

APPENDIX: SAMPLE PAGES OF THE ORIGINAL MANUSCRIPT TO ILLUSTRATE THE AUTHOR'S MIDDLE LOW GERMAN LANGUAGE

Ms. W*3, fol. 116r–117r (ed. Micklin, pp. 241–43; with permission by the publisher, Böhlau. This is the very first part of the text; see Brall-Tuchel, pp. 30–31. I spell the long-shafted 's' this way for pragmatic reasons)

DAr na dat geschreuen is Van dem heilgen lande Vnd van allen landen van ouer mer vnd van Burgen ind van steden, de da ynne gestanden inde noch steint, Nu volget her na, wat Coninge, vursten ind heren vnd patriarchen, Busschouen, ebde, Canoniche vnd paffen ind moniche vnd wilcher hande lude da hant gewont vnd noch wonnent bis vp desen dach, vnd van yrme gelouuen ind partien vnd van all yrme wesen, van krijsten, Joden vnd van heiden.

zo dem eirsten dat Conickrich van Jherusalem liget mytz in der werelde, als man he spricht, vnd dat hat van alders gewest der Joden, vnd dar na was it der krijsten, vnd nu is it der heiden, Mer in dem Conickrich wonnent alre meist krijsten.

Vort van deseme Conickrich intgain dat oisten, da sint alle de Conickrich van Jnida, da is here ouer preister Johan, vnd alle de lude, de da ynne wonnent, de sint krijsten.

Vort intgain dat suyd oyst by Jndia Sint alle Conickrich van Nubien vnd dat Conickrich van Tharsin, vnd de lude sint ouch krijsten, Jnd danne waren Melchior ind Balthasar, zwein van den heilgen drin Coningen, de vnsem heren den offer brachten zo Bethleem.

Vort intgain dat Norden oyst liget dat Conickrich van Georgien vnd dat Conickrich van Abcas, vnd de lude, de da ynne wonnent, sint vrome starcke krijsten.

Vort liget intgain dat norden dat Conickrich van Grecken vnd dat Conickrich van Armenien, vnd de lude, de da wonnent, sint ouch krijsten.

Vort alle dese lude, de in desen Conickrich wonnent, de sint alle krijsten, Mer sy en sint neit al gelich gude krijsten, Sy sint myt etzlichen artikelen ind punten gescheiden vnd gedeilt, als her na geschreuen steit.

Appendix

Vort alle dese Conickrich sint ere yecklich wale so mechtich als der Soldain, Mer dat ir eyn dem anderen neit gelegen en is vur wasser vnd woistenien vnd ander hindernisse.

Vort alle dese krijsten, de in desen landen wonnent, de sint partie, dat erer gein en gelouuet als der ander, de eyne heisschent latini, Surianj, Jndi, Nubiani, Armeni, Greci, Georgiani, Nestorinj, Jacobite, Maroniti, Copti, ysini, Maronini ind Soldini. alle dese partien van krijsten, wa de wonnent, de hant mallich ere sunderliche kirchen, vnd erer gein geit in des anderen kirche noch huys.

Vort preister Johan is krijsten vnd is here ouer Jndien vnd is mechtiger ind meirre here dan der keyser van Rome, vnd wanne hie here wirt ouer Jndien, So wirt eme der name myt, dat hie heist preister Johan, vnd also schrijft he in al synen breuen, Dat hie geynnen groisser ederer hoger name konne gewissen dan eyn preister.

want van eyns preisters macht wirt hemel ind hella vp geslossen vnd zo, vnd wanne eyn preister syn armen vp heuet, So vallent alle keyser vnd Coninge vp ere knee.

Vort de beste stat, de in Jndien liget, de heist Seuwa, da wont preister "Johan", vnd we costlich, riche vnd schone syne pallaese vnd wonningen sint van goulde ind van edelen gesteintze, da were lanck aff zo sprechen, vnd dat en is gein wonder, want man alle dinck da gilt ind vercouft myt papiren zeichen, vnd goult ind syluer, dat blijft zo Cleynnode vnd zo vassen, vnd in alle deme lande van Jndia vnd van Tatteren, da gilt man ind vercouft myt cleynnen stucken van papire, de sint getzeichent dar na, dat sy sint vergulden. [fol. 117r] Jnd wanne eyn man zo vil hette der stucken van papire, de gezeichent weren, de neit lenger geweren end kunden, Dem gift man nuwe stucke vmb de alden ain tol ind weder sprache.

BIBLIOGRAPHY OF WORKS CONSULTED

Abdelkawy Sheir, Ahmed Mohamed, *The Prester John Legend Between East and West During the Crusades: Entangled Eastern-Latin Mythical Legacies*. Mediterranean Studies in Late Antiquity and the Middle Ages, 1 (Budapest: Trivent Publishing, 2022).

Aberth, John, *The Black Death: The Great Mortality of 1348–1350: A Brief History with Documents* (Boston, MA: Bedford/St. Martin's, 2005).

Akşit, İlhan, *The History and Architecture of the Hagia Sophia*, trans. Stuart Kline (Istanbul: Akşit Kültür Turizm Sanat Ajans, 2014).

Althoff, Gerd, *Die Macht der Rituale: Symbolik und Herrschaft im Mittelalter* (Darmstadt: Primus Verlag, 2003).

Antoniou, Jim, *Historical Cairo: A Walk Through the Islamic City* (Cairo: The American University in Cairo Press, 1998)

Ayalon, David, *Outsiders in the Lands of Islam: Mamluks, Mongols and Eunuchs*. Collected Studies Series, 269 (London: Variorum Repr., 1988).

Balthazar: A Black African King in Medieval and Renaissance Art, ed. Kristen Collins and Bryan C. Keene (Los Angeles, CA: J. Paul Getty Museum, 2023).

Barker, Hannah, *That Most Precious Merchandise: The Mediterranean Trade in Black Sea Slaves, 1260–1500*. The Middle Ages Series (Philadelphia, PA: University of Pennsylvania Press, 2019).

Barker, Juliet R. V., *The Tournament in England: 1100–1400* (Woodbridge: Boydell Press, 1986).

Bauden, Frédéric, "The Sons of al-Nāṣir Muḥammad and the Politics of Puppets: Where Did It All Start?," *Mamluk Studies Review* (Middle East Documentation Center, The University of Chicago) 13.1 (2009): 53–81; online at https://knowledge.uchicago.edu/record/1153?ln=en.

Becker-Huberti, Manfred, *Die Heiligen Drei Könige: Geschichten, Legenden und Bräuche* (Cologne: Greven, 2005).

Behland, Max, *Die Dreikönigslegende des Johannes von Hildesheim: Untersuchungen zur niederrheinischen Übersetzung der Trierer Handschrift 1183/485 mit Textedition und vollständigem Wortformenverzeichnis* (Munich: Wilhelm Fink, 1968).

Benedictow, Ole J., *The Complete History of the Black Death* (Woodbridge, Suffolk: The Boydell Press, 2021).

Berkey, Jonathan Porter, *The Transmission of Knowledge in Medieval Cairo: A Social History of Islamic Education* (Princeton, NJ: Princeton University Press, 2014).

Blok, Josine H., *The Early Amazons: Modern and Ancient Perspectives on a Persistent Myth*. Religions in the Graeco-Roman World, 120 (Leiden and Boston: Brill, 1996).

135

Bibliography of Works Consulted

Borgehammar, Stephan, *How the Holy Cross Was Found: From Event to Medieval Legend*; with an appendix of texts. Bibliotheca theologiae practicae, 47 (Stockholm: Almqvist & Wiksell, 1991).

Buquet, Thierry, "Aspects matériels du don d'animaux exotiquess dans les échanges diplomatiques," *Culture matérielle et contacts diplomatiques entre l'occident latin, Byzance et l'Orient islamique (XIe–XVI s.): Actes du colloque de Liège, 27-28 avril 2015*, ed. Frédéric Bauden. Islamic History and Civilization (Leiden and Boston: Brill, 2021), 177–202; online at: DOI: https://doi.org/10.1163/9789004465381_009.

Buquet, Thierry, *"The Die Geschichte der Mongolen des Hethum von Korykos (1307) in der Rückübersetzung durch Jean le Long 'Traitiez des estas et des conditions de quatorze royaumes de Aise' (1351): kritische Edition mit parallelem Abdruck des lateinischen Manuskripts Wrocław, Biblioteka Uniwersytecka, R 262,"* ed. Sven Dörper. Europäische Hochschulschriften, 13, 236 (Frankfurt a. M., Bern, et al.: Peter Lang, 1998).

Buquet, Thierry, "Gyrfalcon in the Middle Ages: An Exotic Bird of Prey (Western Europe and Near East)," *Falconry in the Mediterranean Context During the Pre-Modern Era*, ed. Charles Burnett and Baudouin Van den Abeele. Bibliotheca Cynegetica, 9 (Geneva: Librarie Droz, 2021), 79–98.

Chatonnet, Françoise Briquel and Muriel Debié, *The Syriac World. In Search of a Forgotten Christianity*, trans. Jeffrey Haines (2017; New Haven, CT, and London: Yale University Press, 2023).

Clare, Lucien, *Quintaine, la course de bague et le jeu de têtes* (Paris: Ed. du CNRS, 1983).

Classen, Albrecht, "Ägypten im *Niederrheinischen Orientbericht*: ein spätmittelalterlicher Augenzeuge," *Kairoer Germanistische Studien* 25 (2022): 15–27.

Classen, Albrecht, "Anonymous: Niederrheinische Orientbericht [Low Rhenish Report about the Orient]" (1720 words), *The Literary Encyclopedia*. First published on August 24, 2022 [https://www.litencyc.com/php/sworks.php?rec=true&UID=40912, last accessed on August 24, 2022].

Classen, Albrecht, "Assassins, the Crusades, and the Old Man from the Mountains in Medieval Literature: With an Emphasis on The Stricker's *Daniel von dem Blühenden Tal*," *Marginal Figures in the Global Middle Ages and the Renaissance*, ed. Meg Lota Brown. Arizona Studies in the Middle Ages and the Renaissance, 47 (Turnhout: Brepols, 2021), 123–40.

Classen, Albrecht, "Blacks in the Middle Ages – What About Racism in the Past? Literary and Art-Historical Reflections," pre-print at https://www.qeios.com/read/KIJP54; comments at: https://www.qeios.com/notifications; *Current Research Journal of Social Sciences and Humanities* 6.1 (2023); online at: https://bit.ly/3MuEQsA.

Classen, Albrecht, "Early Encounters with Buddhism: Some Medieval European Travelogue Authors Offer First Insights into a Foreign Religion. Explorations of an Unchartered Territory," to appear in *The East Asian Journal of Philosophy*, special issue, *Dynamic Encounters between Buddhism and the West*, ed. Laura Langone.

Classen, Albrecht, "Entertainment and Recreation in Medieval Courtly Society: Literary, Historical, and Art-Historical Perspectives," to appear in *Groniek: Historisch Tijdschrift*.

Bibliography of Works Consulted

Classen, Albrecht, *Freedom, Imprisonment, and Slavery in the Pre-Modern World: Cultural-Historical, Social-Literary, and Theoretical Reflections.* Fundamentals of Medieval and Early Modern Culture, 25 (Berlin and Boston: Walter de Gruyter, 2021).

Classen, Albrecht, "Global History in the Middle Ages: A Medieval and an Early Modern Perspective. The *Niederrheinische Orientbericht* (c. 1350) and Adam Olearius's *Vermehrte New Beschreibung der Muscowitischen vnd Persischen Reyse* (1647; 1656)," *Philological Quarterly* 100.2 (2021): 101–34.

Classen, Albrecht, "Globalism in the Late Middle Ages: The Low German *Niederrheinische Orientbericht* as a Significant Outpost of a Paradigm Shift. The Move Away from Traditional Eurocentrism," *Globalism in the Middle Ages and the Early Modern Age: Innovative Approaches and Perspectives*, ed. Albrecht Classen. Fundamentals of Medieval and Early Modern Culture, 27 (Berlin and Boston: Walter de Gruyter, 2023), 381–406.

Classen, Albrecht, "Kulturelle und religiöse Kontakte zwischen dem christlichen Europa und dem buddhistischen Indien während des Mittelalters: Rudolfs von Ems *Barlaam und Josaphat* im europäischen Kontext," *Fabula* 41.3/4 (2000): 203–28.

Classen, Albrecht, "Marco Polo and John Mandeville: The Traveler as Authority Figure, the Real and the Imaginary," *Authorities in the Middle Ages: Influence, Legitimacy, and Power in Medieval Society*, ed. Sini Kangas, Mia Korpiola, and Tuija Aionen. Fundamentals of Medieval and Early Modern Culture, 12 (Berlin and Boston: Walter de Gruyter, 2013), 239–48.

Classen, Albrecht, "Queer Medieval," *Oxford Bibliographies in Literary and Critical Theory*, ed. Eugene O'Brien (New York: Oxford University Press, Sept. 22, 2021); online at: https://www.oxfordbibliographies.com/view/document/obo-9780190221911/obo-9780190221911-0111.xml?rskey=2ZgQVg&result=6&q=Queer#firstMatch.

Classen, Albrecht, "Global Middle Ages: Eastern Wisdom (Buddhistic) Teachings in Medieval European Literature. With a Focus on *Barlaam and Josaphat*," *Humanities and Social Science Research* 4.2 (2021): 10–20; https://doi.org/10.30560/hssr.v4n2p10; or: https://j.ideaspread.org/index.php/hssr/article/view/916.

Classen, Albrecht, *Religious Toleration in the Middle Ages and Early Modern Age: An Anthology of Literary, Theological, and Philosophical Texts* (Berlin: Peter Lang, 2020).

Classen, Albrecht, *Toleration and Tolerance in Medieval and Early Modern European Literature.* Routledge Studies in Medieval Literature and Culture, 8 (New York and London: Routledge, 2018; paperback, 2021).

Classen, Albrecht, "The Topic of Persia in Medieval Literary Imagination, with a Focus on Middle High German Literature," *Ceræ: An Australasian Journal of Medieval and Early Modern Studies* 8 (2021; appeared in 2022): 35–65; https://ceraejournal.com/wp-content/uploads/2022/07/Vol-8-FULL-VOLUME.pdf.

Clear, Matthew J., "Piety and Patronage in the Mediterranean: Sancia of Majorca (1286–1345), Queen of Sicily, Provence and Jerusalem," Ph.D. diss., Falmer, University of Sussex, 2000.

Cluse, Christoph, "Juden am Niederrhein während des Mittelalters: Eine Bilanz," *Jüdisches Leben im Rheinland: Vom Mittelalter bis zur Gegenwart*, ed. Monika Grübel and Georg Mölich (Cologne, Weimar, and Vienna: Böhlau, 2005), 1–27.

Bibliography of Works Consulted

Collins Atlas of Bird Migration: Tracing the Great Journeys of the World's Birds, ed. Jonathan Elphick (London: Harper Collins, 1995).

Cortese, Arabella, *Cilicia as Sacred Landscape in Late Antiquity: A Journey on the Trail of Apostles, Martyrs and Local Saints*. Spätantike – Frühes Christentum – Byzanz, 53. Reihe B: Studien und Perspektiven (Wiesbaden: Reichert Verlag, 2022).

Court Cultures in the Muslim World: Seventh to Nineteenth Centuries, ed. Albrecht Fuess and Jan-Peter Hartung. SOAS/Routledge Studies on the Middle East, 13 (London and New York: Routledge, 2011).

Die Beduinen: Stammesgesellschaften und Nomadismus im Nahen Osten. Akten des I. Symposiums der Max Freiherr von Oppenheim-Stiftung, 17.–18. März 2016 im Rautenstrauch-Joest-Museum, Köln, ed. Gernot Wilhelm. Max-Freiherr-von-Oppenheim-Stiftung: Schriften der Max-Freiherr-von-Oppenheim-Stiftung, 19 (Wiesbaden: Harrassowitz, 2018).

Die Heiligen Drei Könige: Mythos, Kunst und Kult: Katalog zur Ausstellung im Museum Schnütgen, Köln, 25. Oktober 2014–25. Januar 2015, ed. Manuela Beer (Munich: Hirmer, 2014).

Druce, George C., "The Caladrius and Its Legend, Sculptured Upon the Twelfth-Century Doorway of Alne Church, Yorkshire," *Archaeological Journal* 69 (1912): 381–416.

Elverskog, Johan, *The Precious Summary: A History of the Mongols from Chinggis Khan to the Qing Dynasty* (New York: Columbia University Press, 2023).

Ennen, L[eonard], "Der Orient: Ein Bericht vom Niederrhein aus dem Ende des 14. Jahrhunderts," *Orient und Occident insbesondere in ihren gegenseitigen Beziehungen: Forschungen und Mittheilungen* 1, ed. Theodor Benfey (Göttingen: Dieterich, 1862), 449–80, and 627–46; online at: https://books.google.com/books?id=Hy0JAAAAQAAJ&pg=PA466&lpg=PA466&dq=Agartini&source=bl&ots=sZFFfIOwiC&sig=ACfU3U0dv0hKC0PqcyttuOZrRdsP4HsE-JA&hl=en&sa=X&ved=2ahUKEwiymbW7-ob6AhU7LUQIHeizAHMQ6AF-6BAgbEAM#v=onepage&q=Agartini&f=false.

Favereau, Marie, *The Horde: How the Mongols Changed the World* (Cambridge, MA, and London: The Belknap Press of Harvard University Press, 2021).

Foss, Clive, *Ephesus After Antiquity: A Late Antique, Byzantine, and Turkish City* (Cambridge: Cambridge University Press, 1979).

Gaunt, Simon, *Marco Polo's Le devisement du monde: Narrative Voice, Language and Diversity*. Gallica, 31 (2013; Cambridge: D. S. Brewer, 2018).

Gautier d'Arras, *Eracle*, ed. and trans. by Karen Pratt. King's College London Medieval Studies, XXI (London: King's College London; Centre for Late Antique & Medieval Studies, 2007).

Germanica Judaica, ed. Zvi Avneri. Vol. II: *Von 1238 bis zur Mitte des 14.* Jahrhunderts (Tübingen: J. C. B. Mohr, 1968).

Glaser, Elvira, "Schweizer Kochbuchhandschriften im spätmittelalterlichen-frühneuzeitlichen Kulturkontakt," *Cibo e salute nelle tradizioni germaniche medievali / Food and Health in the Germanic Middle Ages*, ed. Chiara Benati and Claudia Händl. *Filologia Germanica / Germanic Philology*, Supplemento 3 (Milan: Prometheus, 2022), 119–39.

Bibliography of Works Consulted

Gottfried von Strassburg, *Tristan and Isolde* with Ulrich von Türheim's *Continuation*, ed. and trans., with an intro. by William T. Whobrey (Indianapolis, IN, and Cambridge: Hackett Publishing, 2020).

Griffith, Sidney, "'Melkites', 'Jacobites' and the Christological Controversies in Arabic in Third/Ninth-Century Syria," *Syrian Christians under Islam, the First Thousand Years*, ed. David Thomas (Leiden and Boston: Brill, 2001), 9–55.

Grotefend, H., *Taschenbuch der Zeitrechnung des deutschen Mittelalters und der Neuzeit*. 11th ed., ed. Th. Ulrich (Hanover: Hahnsche Buchhandlung, 1971).

Hächler, Nikolas, "Heraclius Constantine III – Emperor of Byzantium (613–641)," *Byzantinische Zeitschrift* 115.1 (2022): 69–116.

Halabi, Abbas, *The Druze: A New Cultural and Historical Appreciation* (Reading: Ithaca Press, 2015).

Harbus, Antonina, *Helena of Britain in Medieval Legend* (Woodbridge, Suffolk, and Rochester, NY: Brewer, 2002).

Harris, Sylvia C., "German Translations of the 'Historia trium regum' by Johannes von Hildesheim," *The Modern Language Review* 53 (1958): 364–73.

Hayer, Gerold, *Konrad von Megenberg, 'Das Buch der Natur': Untersuchungen zu seiner Text- und Überlieferungsgeschichte*. Münchener Texte und Untersuchungen zur deutschen Literatur des Mittelalters, 110 (Tübingen: Max Niemeyer, 1998).

Hayton, *La flor des estoires de la terre d'Orient*, ed. Charles Kohler, *Recueil des historiens des croisades*. Documents arméniens, 2 (Paris: Imprimerie nationale, 1906), Vol. 2.

Hayton, *Die Geschichte der Mongolen des Hethum von Korykos (1307) in der Rückübersetzung durch Jean le Long "Traitiez des estas et des conditions de quatorze royaumes de Aise" (1351): kritische Edition mit parallelem Abdruck des lateinischen Manuskripts Wrocław, Biblioteka Uniwersytecka, R 262*, ed. Sven Dörper. Europäische Hochschulschriften, 13, 236 (Frankfurt a. M., Bern, et al.: Peter Lang, 1998).

Heng, Geraldine, *Empire of Magic: Medieval Romance and the Politics of Cultural Fantasy* (New York and Chichester: Columbia University Press, 2003).

Heng, Geraldine, *The Invention of Race in the European Middle Ages* (Cambridge: Cambridge University Press, 2018).

Herodot, *Historien*. Two vols. *Griechisch–deutsch*, ed. Josef Feix. 7th ed. Sammlung Tusculum (Berlin: Akademie-Verlag, 2011).

Higgins, Iain Macleod, *Writing East: The "Travels" of Sir John Mandeville*. The Middle Ages Series (Philadelphia, PA: University of Pennsylvania Press, 1997).

Hoch, Adrian S., "Sovereignity and Closure in Trecento Naples: Images of Queen Sancia, alias 'Sister Clare'," *Arte medievale / Istituto della Enciclopedia Italiana* (Milan) 2. Ser. 10.1 (1997): 121–39.

Holt, P. M., "Al Nāṣir Muḥammad," *The Encyclopedia of Islam*. New Edition, ed. C. E. Bosworth, E. van Donzel, et al. Vol. VII (Leiden and New York: E. J. Brill, 1993), 991–93.

Honegger, Thomas, *From Phoenix to Chauntecleer: Medieval English Animal Poetry*. Schweizer anglistische Arbeiten, 120 (Tübingen: Francke, 1996).

Howard-Johnston, James, *The Last Great War of Antiquity* (Oxford: Oxford University Press, 2021).

Incarceration and Slavery in the Middle Ages and Early Modern Age: A Cultural-Historical Investigation of the Dark Side in the Pre-Modern World, ed. Albrecht Classen. Studies in Medieval Literature (Lanham, Boulder, New York, and London: Lexington Books, 2021).

Invitation to Syriac Christianity. An Anthology, ed. Michael Philip Penn, Scott Fitzgerald Johnson, Christine Shepardson, and Charles M. Stang (Oakland, CA: University of California Press, 2022).

Irwin, Robert, *Mamluks and Crusaders: Men of the Sword and Men of the Pen* (Farnham: Ashgate, 2010).

Jahn, Bruno, "Niederrheinische Orientbericht," *Deutsches Literatur-Lexikon: Das Mittelalter*, ed. Wolfgang Achnitz. Vol. 3: *Reiseberichte und Geschichtsdichtung* (Berlin and Boston: Walter de Gruyter, 2012), 170–71.

Jean de Mandeville in Europa: neue Perspektiven in der Reiseliteraturforschung, ed. Ernst Bremer and Susanne Röhl. MittelalterStudien, 12 (Paderborn: Wilhelm Fink, 2007).

John of Hildesheim, *The Three Kings of Cologne: An Early English Translation of the Historia trium regum*, ed. C. Horstmann (1886; Millwood, NY: Kraus, 1975); cf. also Sylvia C. Harris, "German Translations of the 'Historia trium regum' by Johannes von Hildesheim," *The Modern Language Review* 53 (1958): 364–73.

Kaegi, Walter E., *Heraclius: Emperor of Byzantium* (Cambridge: Cambridge University Press, 2003).

Kleinbauer, W. Eugene and Anthony White, *Hagia Sophia* (London: Scala Publishers, 2007).

Klueting, Edeltraut, "*Quis fuerit Machometus?* Mohammed im lateinischen Mittelalter (11.–13. Jahrhundert," *Archiv für Kulturgeschichte* 90 (2008): 283–306.

Köbler, Gerhard, *Mittelniederdeutsches Wörterbuch*, 3rd ed., 2014, online at: https://www.koeblergerhard.de/mnd/mnd_a.html.

Konrad von Megenberg, *Das Buch der Natur*. Vol. II: *Kritischer Text nach den Handschriften*, ed. Robert Luff and Georg Steer (Tübingen: Max Niemeyer, 2003).

Külzer, Andreas, "Ephesos in byzantinischer Zeit: ein historischer Überblick," *Byzanz – das Römerreich im Mittelalter*. Part 2.2: *Schauplätze: Byzantium – the Roman Empire in the Middle Ages*, ed. Falko Daim and Jörg Drauschke. Römisch-Germanisches Zentralmuseum: Monographien, 84 (Mainz: Römisch-Germanisches Zentralmuseum, 2011), 31–49.

Lach, Donald F. and Edwin J. Van Kley, *Asia in the Making of Europe*. Vol. III: *A Century of Advance, Book Four, East Asia* (Chicago: University of Chicago Press, 1994).

Lacour, Paul, *Les Amazones*. Les femmes dans l'histoire (Paris: Perrin, 1901).

Laffaye, Horace A., *The Polo Encyclopedia*. 2nd ed. (2004; Jefferson, NC: McFarlane, 2015).

Lahaye-Geusen, Maria, *Das Opfer der Kinder: ein Beitrag zur Liturgie- und Sozialgeschichte des Mönchtums im Hohen Mittelalter*. Münsteraner theologische Abhandlungen, 13 (Altenberge: Oros-Verlag, 1991).

Lendinara, Patrizia, "Food Miracles in the Early Lives of St Cuthbert," *Cibo e salute nelle tradizioni germaniche medievali / Food and Health in the Germanic Middle Ages*, ed. Chiara Benati and Claudia Händl. *Filologia Germanica / Germanic Philology*, Supplemento 3 (Milan: Prometheus, 2022), 189–223.

Bibliography of Works Consulted

Levanoni, Amalia, *A Turning Point in Mamluk History: The Third Reign of Al-Nāṣir Muḥammad Ibn Qalāwūn (1310–1341)*. Islamic History and Civilization, 10 (Leiden and Boston: Brill, 1995).

Making Cairo Medieval, ed. Nezar AlSayyad, Irene A. Biermann, and Nasser Rabbat. Transnational Perspectives on Space and Place (Lanham, MD: Lexington Books, 2005).

The Mamluks in Egyptian Politics and Society, ed. Thomas Philipp and Ulrich Haarmann. Cambridge Studies in Islamic Civilization (Cambridge: Cambridge University Press, 1998).

Mandeville, *Le livre de Jean de Mandeville*. Éd. bilingue, établie, traduite, présentée et annotée par Michèle Guéret-Laferté et Laurence Harf-Lancner. Champion Classiques. Série "Moyen Âge", 57 (Paris: Champion Classiques, Honoré Champion, 2023).

Mayor, Adrienne, *The Amazons: Lives and Legends of Warrior Women Across the Ancient World* (Princeton, NJ: Princeton University Press, 2014).

Medieval Latin Lives of Muhammad, ed. and trans. Julian Yolles and Jessica Weiss (Cambridge, MA: Harvard University Press, 2018).

Mehler, N., "The Export of Gyrfalcons from Iceland During the 16th Century: A Boundless Business in a Proto-Globalized World," *Raptor and Human: Falconry and Bird Symbolism Throughout the Millennia on a Global Scale*, ed. K.-H. Gersmann and O. Grimme. Advanced Studies on the Archaeology and History of Hunting, 1.1 (Kiel and Hamburg: Wachholtz, 2018), vol. 3, 995–1020.

Micklin, Anja, *Der »Niederrheinische Orientbericht«: Edition und sprachliche Untersuchung*. Rheinisches Archiv, 163 (Vienna, Weimar, and Cologne: Böhlau, 2021).

Mielke, Andreas, *Nigra sum et Formosa: Afrikanerinnen in der deutschen Literatur des Mittelalters. Texte und Kontexte zum Bild des Afrikaners in der literarischen Imagologie*. Helfant Texte, T 11 (Stuttgart: helfant edition, 1992).

Morton, Nicholas, *The Crusader States and Their Neighbours: A Military History, 1099–1187* (Oxford: Oxford University Press, 2020).

Musto, Ronald G., *Queen Sancia of Naples (1281–1345) and the Spiritual Franciscans in Women of the Medieval World* (Oxford: Basil Blackwell, 1985).

Odorico da Pordenone, *Relatio de Mirabilibus Orientalium Tatarorum*. Edizione critica a cura di Annalia Marchisio (Florence: SISMEL, Edizioni del Galluzzo, 2016).

Orality and Literacy in the Middle Ages: Essays on a Conjunction and its Consequences in Honour of D. H. Green, ed. Mark Chinca and Christopher Young. Utrecht Studies in Medieval Literacy, 12 (Turnhout: Brepols, 2005).

Pandemic Disease in the Medieval World: Rethinking the Black Death, ed. Monica H. Green (Kalamazoo, MI: Arc Medieval Press, 2015).

Park, Sool, *Paradoxien der Grenzsprache und das Problem der Übersetzung. Eine Studie zur Textualität philosophischer Texte und zu historischen Übersetzungsstrategien* (Würzburg: Königshausen & Neumann, 2022).

Patrick, Geary J., *Women at the Beginning: Origin Myths from the Amazons to the Virgin Mary* (Princeton, NJ: Princeton University Press, 2006).

The Phoenix, ed. N. F. Blake. Old and Middle English Texts (Manchester: Manchester University Press, 1964).

Pipes, Daniel, *Slave Soldiers and Islam: The Genesis of a Military System* (New Haven, CT: Yale University Press, 1981).

Bibliography of Works Consulted

Polo, Marco, *Le Devisement du monde*, ed. critique de Philippe Ménard. 6 vols. Textes Littéraires Français (Geneva: Librairie Droz, 2001–2009).

Polo, Marco, *Travels*, trans. and with an intro. by Ronald Latham (London: Penguin, 1958).

Polo, Marco, *The Travels of Marco Polo the Venetian*, with an intro. by John Masefield (1931; New Delhi: Chennai, 2003), online at https://books.google.com/books?id=AP7pPgFfyB4C&pg=PA135&lpg=PA135&dq=erginul&source=bl&ots=gs1od5x-ug&sig=ACfU3U1EaGG1a4MPk3qdQvl9euCb-Q7IRuA&hl=en&sa=X&ved=2ahUKEwizuavqsPT5AhWYL0QIHUG7Dn-4Q6AF6BAgVEAM#v=onepage&q=erginul&f=false, ch. LII, 135–36.

Pratt, Karen, "The Genre of Gautier d'Arras's Eracle: A Twelfth-Century French 'History' of a Byzantine Emperor," *Reading Medieval Studies* XXXIV (2008):169-90; online at: https://www.reading.ac.uk/gcms/-/media/project/functions/research/graduate-centre-for-medieval-studies/documents/rms200811-k-pratt-the-genre-of-gautier-darrass-eracle.pdf?la=en&hash=F262D48710A6618D949716E3CDBDBCF8.

Pratt, Karen, *Meister Otte's Eraclius as an Adaptation of Eracle by Gautier d'Arras*. Göppinger Arbeiten zur Germanistik, 392 (Göppingen: Kümmerle Verlag, 1987).

Prester John: The Legend and its Sources, compiled and trans. by Keagan Brewer. Crusade Texts in Translation, 27 (Farnham: Ashgate, 2015).

Raj, Danuta, Katarzyna Pękacka-Falkowska, Maciej Włodarczyk, and Jakub Węglorz, "The Real Theriac – Panacea, Poisonous Drug or Quackery?," *J Ethnopharmacol* 281 (2021 Dec. 5:114535. doi: 10.1016/j.jep.2021.114535. Epub 2021 Aug. 17.

Rappole, John H., *The Avian Migrant: The Biology of Bird Migration* (New York: Columbia University Press, 2013).

Raymond, André, *Arabic Cities in the Ottoman Period: Cairo, Syria and the Maghreb*. Variorum Collected Studies Series (Aldershot, Hampshire, and Burlington, VT: Ashgate, 2002).

Reichstein, Frank-Michael, *Das Beginenwesen in Deutschland. Studien und Katalog*. Wissenschaftliche Schriftenreihe Geschichte. Band 9. 2nd ed. (Berlin: Verlag Dr. Köster, 2017).

Reliquientranslation und Heiligenverehrung: Symposion zum 850jährigen Anniversarium der Dreikönigstranslation 1164; 24. Oktober 2014, ed. Heinz Finger. Libelli Rhenani, 60 (Cologne: Erzbischöfliche Diözesan- und Dombibliothek, 2015).

Röhricht, Reinhold and Heinrich Meisner, "Ein niederrheinischer Bericht über den Orient," *Zeitschrift für deutsche Philologie* 19 (1887): 1–86.

Rough Cilicia: New Historical and Archaeological Approaches: Proceedings of an International Conference held at Lincoln, Nebraska, October 2007, ed. Michael C. Hoff and Rhys F. Townsend (Oxford: Oxbow Books, 2013).

Roussel, Cyril, *Les Druzes de Syrie*. Contemporain publications, 31 (Beirut : Presses de l'Ifpo, 2011).

Rüther, A., "Oblate," *Lexikon des Mittelalters* vol. VI: *Lukasbilder bis Plantagenêt* (Munich and Zürich: Artemis & Winkler Verlag, 1993), 1336–37.

Schiller, Karl and August Lübben, *Mittelniederdeutsches Wörterbuch*. Fotomechanischer Neudruck der Ausgabe 1875– (Vaduz, Liechtenstein: Sändig-Repr.-Verlag

Wohlwend, 1968–); online at: https://www.koeblergerhard.de/Fontes/Luebben_MittelniederdeutschesHandwoerterbuch1888.pdf.

Schmitz-Esser, Romedio, "The Buddha and the Medieval West: Changing Perspectives on Cultural Exchange between Asia and Europe in the Middle Ages," *Travel, Time, and Space in the Middle Ages and Early Modern Time: Explorations of World Perceptions and Processes of Identity Formation*, ed. Albrecht Classen. Fundamentals of Medieval and Early Modern Culture, 22 (Berlin and Boston: Walter de Gruyter, 2018), 311–30.

Scholz, Manfred Günter, *Hören und Lesen: Studien zur primären Rezeption der Literatur im 12. und 13. Jahrhundert* (Wiesbaden: Steiner, 1980).

Schrader, Helena P., *The Holy Land in the Era of the Crusades: Kingdoms at the Crossroads of Civilizations, 1100–1300* (Barnsley: Pen & Sword History, 2022).

Simons, Walter, *Cities of Ladies: Beguine Communities in the Medieval Low Countries, 1200–1565*. The Middle Ages Series (Philadelphia, PA: University of Pennsylvania Press, 2001).

Slavery and the Slave Trade in the Eastern Mediterranean (c. 1000–1500 CE), ed. Reuven Amitai and Christoph Cluse. Mediterranean Nexus 1100–1700, 5 (Turnhout: Brepols, 2018).

Sourcebook in the Mathematics of Medieval Europe and North Africa, ed. Victor J. Katz, Menso Folkerts, Barnabas Hughes, Roi Wagner, and J. Lennart Berggren (Princeton, NJ, and Oxford: Princeton University Press, 2016).

Sprachgeschichte vor Ort: Stadtsprachenforschung im Spannungsfeld zwischen Ortspunkt und Sprachraum, ed. Matthias Schulz and Lukas Kütt (Heidelberg: Universitätsverlag Winter, 2022).

Spriewald, Ingeborg, *Literatur zwischen Hören und Lesen: Wandel von Funktion und Rezeption im späten Mittelalter. Fallstudien zu Beheim, Folz und Sachs* (Berlin: Aufbau-Verlag, 1990).

Stabler Miller, Tanya, *The Beguines of Medieval Paris: Gender, Patronage, and Spiritual Authority* (Philadelphia, PA: University of Pennsylvania Press, 2014).

Stabler Miller, Tanya, "'More Useful in the Salvation of Others': Beguines, *Religio*, and the *Cura Mulierum* at the Early Sorbonne," *Between Orders and Heresy: Rethinking Medieval Religious Movements*, ed. Jennifer Kolpacoff Deane and Anne E. Lester (Toronto, Buffalo, and London: University of Toronto Press, 2022), 214–41.

Steensen, Thomas, *Die Friesen: Menschen am Meer* (Kiel and Hamburg: Wachholtz, 2020).

The Syriac World, ed. Daniel King. The Routledge World (London and New York: Routledge, 2019).

Tolan, John V., *Faces of Muhammad: Western Perceptions of the Prophet of Islam from the Middle Ages to Today* (Princeton, NJ: Princeton University Press, 2019).

Tolan, John V., *Sons of Ishmael: Muslims Through European Eyes in the Middle Ages* (2008; Gainesville, Tallahassee, et al., FL: University Press of Florida, 2013).

Tolan, John, Gilles Veinstein, and Henry Laurens, *Europe and the Islamic World: A History*, trans. by Jane Marie Todd (Princeton, NJ, and Oxford: Princeton University Press, 2013).

Travel, Time, and Space in the Middle Ages and Early Modern Time: Explorations of Worldly Perceptions and Processes of Identity Formation, ed. Albrecht Classen.

Fundamentals of Medieval and Early Modern Culture, 22 (Berlin and Boston: Walter de Gruyter, 2018).

Tzanaki, Rosemary, *Mandeville's Medieval Audiences: A Study on the Reception of the Book of Sir John Mandeville (1371–1550)* (Aldershot, Hampshire: Ashgate, 2003).

Unwin, Mike and David Tipling, *Flights of Passage: An Illustrated Natural History of Bird Migration* (New Haven, CT, and London: Yale University Press, 2020).

van den Broek, R., *The Myth of the Phoenix – According to Classical and Early Christian Traditions*. Etudes préliminaires aux religions orientales dans l'empire romain, 24 (Leiden: Brill, 1972).

Van Engen, John, *Sisters and Brothers of the Common Life: The Devotio moderna and the World of the Later Middle Ages*. The Middle Ages Series (Philadelphia, PA: University of Pennsylvania Press, 2008).

Van Jaarsveld, Ernst J. and Eric Judd, *Tree Aloes of Africa* (Cape Town: Penrock Publications, 2015).

Von Christen, Juden und von Heiden: Der niederrheinische Orientbericht, ed., trans., and commentary by Helmut Brall-Tuchel. Unter Mitarbeit von Jana Katczynski, Verena Rheinberg, and Sarafina Yamoah (Göttingen: V& R unipress, 2019).

von den Brincken, Anna-Dorothee, *Die 'Nationes Christianorum Orientalium' im Verständnis der lateinischen Historiographie von der Mitte des 12. bis in die zweite Hälfte des 14. Jahrhunderts*. Kölner historische Abhandlungen, 22 (Cologne and Vienna: Böhlau, 1973).

von den Brincken, Anna-Dorothee, "Niederrheinische Orientbericht," *Die deutsche Literatur des Mittelalters: Verfasserlexikon*, ed. Kurt Ruh et al. Vol. 6 (Berlin and New York: Walter de Gruyter, 1987), 998–1000.

Von Widukind zur ›Sassine‹: Prozesse der Konstruktion und Transformation regionaler Identität im norddeutschen Raum, ed. Martin Baisch, Malena Ratzke, and Regina Toepfer. Forschungen zur Kunst, Geschichte und Literatur des Mittelalters, 4 (Vienna and Cologne: Böhlau, 2023).

Wakeley, James Moreton, *At the Origins of Islam: Muḥammad, the Community of the Qurʾān, and the Transformation of the Bedouin World* (Oxford, Bern, Berlin, et al.: Peter Lang, 2022).

Walters Dols, Michael, *The Black Death in the Middle East* (Princeton, NJ: Princeton University Press, 2019).

Watson, Gilbert, *Theriac and Mithridatium: A Study in Therapeutics*. Publications of the Welcome Historical Medical Library, N.S., 9 (London: The Welcome Histor. Med. Library, 1966).

Werner, Roberta, *Reaching for God: The Benedictine Oblate Way of Life* (Collegeville, MN: Liturgical Press, 2013).

Western Views of Islam in Medieval and Early Modern Europe: Perception of Other, ed. Michael Frassetto and David A. Blanks (1999; New York: Palgrave Macmillan, 2016).

Woebcken, *Das Land der Friesen und seine Geschichte* (1932; Walluf b. Wiesbaden: Sändig, 1973).

INDEX

This index covers the Introduction and the primary text, but not the extensive commentary.

Aaron   38
Abkhazia   17
Abraham   56
Acre   26, 37, 46, 63, 64, 71
Adam's apple   77
Ahasuerus   56, 57, 58
Alexander the Great   38, 54, 55, 58
Alexandria   20
Altelot   49, 50
Andalusia   1
St Andrew   50
antelope   67
St Anthony   18
Antioch   49, 50
Arabians (horses)   45
Aragon   80
Armenia, Armenians   4, 7, 10, 17, 23, 24, 25, 26, 27, 46, 52, 53, 55, 71
Arnold von Harff   9
asparagus   78

Babyon   22, 24, 33, 37, 49, 56, 75
Baghdad   55, 56
ball games   45
Balthazar   20, 54, 58
St Barbara   27, 46
Bartholomew Anglicus   6
belech   68–69
Bernhard von Breydenbach   6
Bethlehem   17, 21
bezants   64, 79
Black Death   13
broom   81
Bruder Philipp   9
Brunzilia wood   77
buffalo   69
Byzantine civil war   13

Cairo   14, 38
Cambeloch   55, 56
camel   70
Candelot   49

cannibals   59
caradrius   75
carob   78
Cathay   54
cedar tree   76
cherries   80
chickens   75
St Christopher   59
Cologne   2, 4, 10, 13, 14, 26
Constantinople   23, 24, 49, 51
Copts   17, 21
cotton   78
cranes   19, 43, 44, 45, 59, 73
crocodile   71
cypress   76

Damascus   25, 37, 39, 41, 48, 49
dancing   40
Darius   54
dates   76
dogs   3, 20, 33, 34, 39, 40, 43, 44, 54, 57, 58, 63, 64, 68, 69, 71, 72, 73
dragon   70
dromedary   71

eagle   73
earthquakes   61
Edwardian War   4
Egypt   20, 21, 22, 24, 37, 38, 43, 44, 48, 61, 71
elephants   43, 44, 57, 66, 69, 70, 71
Ellen   62
entertainment   40
Eraclius of Cosdras   48
Eraclius/Heraclius, Emperor   39, 48
Ethiopians   17
Euphrates   54, 56

falcons/falconry   18, 39, 40, 43, 44, 46, 56, 58, 75, 76
Felix Fabri   9
flamingo   74

Index

Flanders 75, 81
fox 59
francolin 74
French 6, 56, 62, 64

galangal ginger *see* ginger
Gaza (king of) 37, 39, 47
Geoffrey of Bouillon 50
Georgia 4, 7, 17, 22, 23, 24
Georgians 17
ginger 80
giraffe 69
goat 68
grapefruit 80
Great Khan 54
Greece, Greeks 17

Hagia Sophia 51
Halaam 52, 54
harem 41
hazelnut 80
Hethum 55
honey 79–80
horse/s 5, 23, 45, 47, 48, 52, 54, 64, 66,
    71, 72, 74
Hundred Years' War 4, 14, 51

Ibn Battuta 1
Ibn Fadlan 1
Ibn Jubayr 1
incense 80
India, Indians 1, 5, 7, 17, 18, 19, 20, 27,
    37, 40, 54, 56, 60, 64, 67, 69, 70,
    72, 75, 80

Jacobites 17, 21
Jew/s 3, 4, 7, 14, 17, 21, 22, 26, 29, 30,
    32, 35, 39, 41, 42, 46, 48, 50, 52,
    55, 66, 80
Johannes von Hildesheim 9
John Mandeville 1, 10
St John 51
Joseph 34, 38
Joshua 80

Khan 56
Konrad von Megenberg 5
Konrad von Würzburg 9

Latins 17
leopards 39, 66, 67, 68, 71, 72, 73
library 46–47
lime 77
lions 58, 66, 67

St Macarius 18
magpie 53
make-up 62
Mamluks 12, 14
Marco Polo 1, 5, 10
Maronians 17, 22 (probably the same as
    Maronites)
Maronites 17, 21
Mary 30, 34
Meister Wichwolt 9
Melchior 17, 20
mercenaries 47
Mesopotamia 54
Messina 51
money 53
Mongolia 51
Morant und Galie 9
Moses 29, 30, 38

Nebuchadnezza 55, 58
Nestorians 6, 17, 21
Nicodemus 21
Nile 43, 44, 71, 77
Nineveh 54
Norway 75
Nubia, Nubians 17, 20, 21
Nutmeg 80

Odorico da Pordenone 5
orange 77
Orthosa 50
ostrich 73

palm tree 76
panther 67
Paradise 19, 20, 30, 31, 33, 54, 56, 58,
    59, 71, 76, 77
Paradise apples 77
parrot 74
partridges 76
pelican 74
pepper 78
Persia, Persians 5, 6, 7, 28, 30, 60, 61
St Peter 21, 50, 59
St Petronilla 49
Pharaoh figs 78
phoenix 75
pigeons 75
pistachios 78
pomelo 80
Prester John 17, 18, 19, 20, 21, 54
Prussia 75

quail (common) 74

146

Index

Queen of Saba   48

ram   68
Rhine   2
rice   78

saffron   80
salamander   68
Saleff   49
Satalia   49, 50
scarlet   81
Schalbonnire   49
Seelentrost / Kleiner Seelentrost   9
shoes   25, 42, 62
Shrovetide   76
Sichki   49
Sicily   1
sikkim tree   77
singing   40
Spain   1, 47, 48, 66, 72
sparrow falcons   75
storks   75
sugar, sugar cane   79
Susa   56, 57
Syrians   17
swallows   75

Tartars   51, 52, 53, 54

Tenghes   47
Thauris   *see* Susa
St Thomas   20
Thomas de Cantimpré   5
Thomas, Patriarch   18
thyme   80
tiger   67
Tigris   54
Tunisia   1

unicorn   67

Venice   66, 72
Vincent of Beauvais   5
Vistula cherries   80
Vitae Patrum   72

wildcat   71
wine   25, 31, 34, 35, 36, 51, 63, 70, 74
wolf   59, 71

Xerxes   58

Yāqūt Shihāb al-Dīn ibn-ʿAbdullāh
        al-Rūmī al-Ḥamawī   1

Zabalin   51

Printed in the USA
CPSIA information can be obtained
at www.ICGtesting.com
CBHW051159111024
15704CB00004B/226